ALCOHOL AMONG YOUNG PEOPLE:

obtaining the full measure

GODFREY HOLMES

Published by the Boys' and Girls' Welfare Society 1990
Schools Hill, Cheadle, Cheshire SK8 1JE.

Typeset & printed by Manchester Free Press
Paragon Mill, Jersey Street, Manchester M4 6FP. 061-236 8822.

ISBN 1 869801 07 5

Registered Charity No. 209782.

Front cover courtesy of *The Guardian*

THE PUBLISHER

The Boys' and Girls' Welfare Society is an independent charitable organisation which was founded in 1870 in Manchester. Since that time it has maintained a prominent and important role in the social and educational care of children and young people. It is actively concerned with the needs of children and young people in society, the family, and the school.

The major aims of the Society are:—

To provide appropriate residential care and education for deprived, disadvantaged, handicapped or emotionally disturbed children and young people.

To provide, assist, or participate in community based care and education projects for the benefit of the deprived, disadvantaged, and/or handicapped in society.

To initiate and promote research and publication in the field of social and educational care.

To promote and participate in complementary co-operative ventures in social work and education.

To improve professional standards in those caring professions concerned with children and young people.

"I was glad when they said unto me
Let us go out of this place. . ."

to

DR. PAUL WILDING

Professor of Social Policy at the University

of Manchester

* * * * * * * * * * *

My Tutor 1967 onwards. . .

* * * * * * * * * * *

"Then I saw that wisdom excels folly

as light excels darkness."

(Ecclesiastes 2: v.12)

ACKNOWLEDGEMENTS

First I should like to acknowledge the invaluable contribution of the Department of Youth Work at Manchester University, and its then Head of Studies Dr. Cyril Smith, for introducing me to the study of adolescence, and to the work of the Manchester Youth Development Trust.

Second, I should pay tribute to Ric Rogers, for ten years Editor of "Youth In Society" (the magazine of The National Youth Bureau). He encouraged me to write the article: *In Praise of Tearaways*, in July 1986, that formed the outline for this book.

Third, I should thank BBC1, and the editor of *Panorama* in particular, for kindly sending me the transcript of the documentary screened on Monday 12th October 1987 *Heroin: More Harm than Heroin*. That programme was a landmark in the exploration of alcohol among young people. Remaining with broadcasters, my thanks to Brook Productions and Channel 4 for the information contained in 2 programmes broadcast on January 2nd, 1990 and January 9th, 1990: *Drink — Brewing Trouble*, followed by: *Drink — Under the Influence* — and for supplying the booklet "DRINK" tied in with those transmissions. The University of Aston also sent me recent research which I found invaluable.

Fourth, my gratitude to Michael J. Ring of INSCRIBE GRAPHICS of Nottingham, for designing the frontispiece: "I was glad...", and to Franklin Watts Publishers for allowing me to reprint an illustration from *Alcohol Abuse* by Brian Ward.

Fifth, I have a specific debt to the Boys' and Girls' Welfare Society, to its Chief Executive, John McMaster, and to its Senior Administrative Assistant, Susan Lamonby for enabling me to complete this project, and for arranging proofs and layout.

Sixth, my colleagues at Chilwell Comprehensive School, and later in North-East and North-West Nottingham Social Services' supplied me with advice, material, observations and constructive criticism. My current employers, Derbyshire County Council have shown much interest in my writing, and have also helped me to make space for it. This I acknowledge.

Lastly, I wish to thank my parents who sadly are no longer alive, and my wife Janet who is very much alive, for their special contribution. My father, Revd. Arthur J. Holmes had very clear views about citizenship in general, and alcohol in particular — views he shared with me, and sermons which he preached. Some of the choruses I quote preceded even his long ministry.

Godfrey Holmes

CONTENTS

INTRODUCTION

Stop, ere you lift the brimming cup!
Pause, ere it touch your lip!
You may not fear its blighting power
As you its richness sip:
But are there none who see the act
Whom it may lead to harm;
Some who, if once they taste the draught,
Can ne'er break from its charm?

from the Temperance Melodist, 1891

Before privatisation, water suddenly began to advertise itself. Nightly, television screens showed milk floats trundling round housing estates loaded with all the water families might require. The image was of a great jet of water: powerful enough to wash cars, to clean factories, to irrigate fields, to cool molten steel, even to disperse riotous crowds!

Presumably the water authorities wished to draw attention to a God-given product which most of the population had hitherto taken for granted. What would happen if the tap ever ran dry? — was the underlying message.

In tackling the subject of alcohol, one of the difficulties is the **universality** of alcohol. Alcohol is taken for granted. The beer pump goes on pumping. The wine press goes on pressing. The still goes on distilling. The tap does not run dry.

Alcohol is the backdrop of adult life: part of the drama on and off stage, part of work, part of unemployment, part of holidaying, part of staying at home, part of socialising, part of being antisocial, part of celebrating, part of grieving, part of hoping, part of giving up hope.

In a society now more dedicated to leisure, alcohol beats even the gramophone record, the camera, the videotape, and the automobile as the ideal leisure product: cheap, brightly packaged, heavily advertised, widely coveted — yet so accessible. In many ways, alcohol **is** leisure for it can accompany or underpin all other leisure.

Where lifestyle matters, alcohol matters — because alcohol, even abstinence from alcohol, is the badge of lifestyle. Alcohol is the way to be recognised, the mystery key to open every door that might otherwise remain firmly shut.

It follows that **young people** will be especially intrigued by alcohol. They are maturing and merging into adulthood. Inasmuch as the machinery of adulthood relies upon the lubrication of alcohol, teenagers will examine the machinery, take some parts out, rearrange other parts to suit their own personalities, and then they will top up with more alcohol!

Surprisingly little has been written about alcohol among young people. Yet there is a vast library on the subject of alcohol and alcohol-dependence in general. Teenage drinking goes on in a dimly lit corner of people's awareness. Anybody who **does** write about alcohol among young people must have something to say specifically about youth. No advantage is to be gained simply by producing another guide to alcohol with every reference to men and women struck out in favour of references to boys and girls, young men and young women.

Throughout, the thrust of my discussion will address the question of alcohol among people 18 years and younger. However, because most of the available statistics, and nearly all the influences, extend to the age band 19 to 24, young adults below the age of 25 will often be mentioned. That ties in neatly with the (illogical) definition of a young person used by the Department of Social Security: a "child" 24 years of age or under: the full length of an apprenticeship in the Seventeenth Century.

The writer must also be able to move beyond ascertaining **how much** alcohol young people drink. That is an important starting-point, but other questions are what beverages young people are consuming, where, with whom, and with what consequences. The tableau provides what a meter cannot.

The most insidious snare to be avoided is "medicalisation" of the subject of young people's drinking habits: that is, handing the subject over to medical practitioners, leaving it on the surgery counter sure that the doctor can "do something about it" — maybe without the need to go back.

Alcohol among young people is not alcohol among **sick** young people who will be **cured** if they accept **treatment**. Yes, alcohol does make inroads into good health, but alcohol is too restless, too irrepressible, to be confined to bed. Everybody can comment on alcohol. Everybody can observe. Everybody can intervene.

Having said that, two of the best texts are produced by doctors: *Alcohol and Alcoholism*, a Report from the Royal College of Psychiatrists, and *Alcohol Problems* by Peter Anderson, Paul Wallace and Heather Jones — and readers are warmly commended to imbibe these.

The pure alcoholic content of any strong drink is a volume percentage. In succeeding chapters, the words "alcohol", "drink", and "drinking" are frequently used in their colloquial sense. It is a great pity that the simple word Drink has been hi-jacked to mean (mainly) strong drink, but that usage is very old, very well-established, and not worth setting aside in the interests of pedantry.

Appendix One will carry discussion away from young people to the sight of their parents and guardians drinking.

Other Appendices deal specifically with the 'lager lout' phenomenon and with advertising alcohol. These Appendices should be read as part of the main book, because the three areas cover themes relevant to all six chapters.

CHAPTER ONE

Discovering the Extent

"I'm very fond of a social glass."
"So am I."
"So am I."
"It makes the time so pleasantly pass,
And fills the heart with pleasure."
"Ah, water pure doth brighter shine
Than brandy, rum, or sparkling wine."
"But sad is the fix if the liquors you mix."
"Oh I never do that."
"Nor do I."
"Nor do I."

from the Temperance Melodist, 1891

Historical Factors

Undoubtedly young people now drink less than they did 100 years ago. Or even 200 years ago. Indeed, it is estimated that per capita levels of consumption (averaged across the whole population, including children) were four times higher in 1680 than present levels.

By the Eighteenth Century, tea drinking had become more popular — but consumption of ale, mead and gin accompanied the onset of the Industrial Revolution. The notorious Beer Act of 1830 was intended to lessen the impact of spirits, but had the side effect of vastly increasing the number of beer-shops. For every one beer-shop that had existed before the Act, 250 opened within a six-month period. Anybody could obtain a licence to sell beer for the modest fee of two guineas.

During the last century, many publicans offered sweets and toys, even cheap cigarettes, as an inducement to children to bring their parents to an inn. One quarter of all public house customers in 1897 were infants or children under 13 years of age. An early social survey was staged between 1 and 3pm one Sunday, at a point where two inns stood opposite each other. 285 boy and girl customers were observed with jugs and bottles for out-sales, as well as 230 boys and girls entering without jugs or bottles.

Anxiety about juvenile alcoholism was such that two separate moves began: firstly, to limit publicans' ability to serve young people, and secondly, to encourage young people to join temperance organisations.

A Licensing Act was passed in 1872 despite grave reservations expressed in Parliament, not least by members with brewing interests. A penalty of twenty shillings (one pound) was to be imposed on any publican who sold **spirits** to any person "apparently under the age of 16". In 1886 there followed the Intoxicating Liquors (Sale to Children) Act which forbade the sale of beers or spirits to under 13 year olds **for drinking on licensed premises**. A twenty-shilling fine remained for the first offence, forty shillings for a second offence.

In 1901 Parliament passed a measure known as the Anti-Sipping Act, prohibiting the sale of alcohol to children under the age of 14 where it was to be consumed off the premises. A concession to publicans allowed them to sell liquor to **any** child provided the bottle was sealed in such a way that the seal (usually a paper strip) had to be broken in order to reach the contents. By 1908 Parliament was able to debate a much stronger measure (part of The Children's Charter) making it illegal to have any child under 14 in a bar or in a place used mainly for the serving of alcohol.

Only in 1923 did Lady Astors' Bill make it illegal to serve any kind of intoxicating liquor to anyone apparently under the age of 18 who intended to consume the drink on licensed premises. Even then, the Bill did not outlaw out-sales to young people.

In the light of modern one-issue pressure-groups like C.N.D. and Anti-Vivisection, it is possible to imagine a Temperance Movement that had its heyday in the Victorian Era. It is less possible to envisage **such** a populous and vociferous lobby focussing on "the evil" of strong drink. If present-day nuclear disarmers know their Tridents from their Nimrods, and if Animal Rights' activists know their mechanically-recovered meat from their steroid-treated meat, so very young abstainers were expected to answer questions like:

"In what respects does methylic alcohol differ from ethylic?" and, "What scientific evidence is there that water is an all-sufficient drink?"

The word "Temperance" can mean moderation, but in the context of alcohol it means Total Abstinence (tee-totallism). The most famous branch of the Temperance Movement was The Band of Hope. At the turn of this century, there were 29,000 junior Bands of Hope — one for every four public houses — and 3½ million children went along. The Good Templars, The Rechabites, and the Sons of Temperance also had special branches for young adherents.

The Methodist Church — both before and after Methodist Union in 1932 — was foremost among religious denominations propounding Total Abstinence, and urging young abstainers to "sign the pledge", that is, to renounce consumption of any alcohol for the rest of their lives. The Wesleyan Young Abstainers' League started in 1912 with 8000 members aged between 14 and 21, whilst the Primitive Methodists claimed 59,000 young abstainers by 1914, with 3168 small children enrolled as well. The Primitives had an eventual aim of attracting **every** young Methodist to forsake alcohol. Even then, it was estimated that a half of all Methodist Sunday Schools in the land had no formal link with a temperance society.

With respectable, if not respected, licensing laws; with the passage of two World Wars; with a noticeable decline in young people's religious affiliation; with the attempted removal of drunkenness from the streets; and with the opening up of many cheap new leisure opportunities (like silent movies), the Temperance Movement had lost all its momentum by 1950, the year the Band of Hope counted ¾ of all young people drinking spasmodically or regularly. The focus then switched to young people and cigarettes, rock 'n' roll, motor-scooters, Beatlemania, punk hairstyles, and the menace of hard drugs. The new "teenagers" — short for "between-ages" threw adults off the alcoholic scent.

Some Surveys

Quantifying the extent of latter-day teenage drinking is a hazardous business. There would be little point standing opposite two public houses **now** at Sunday lunchtime adding up all the young people going in and out with assorted vessels. Many children would be about to eat a restaurant meal with their parents, in which case they can legally be served alcohol, and others would be the waitresses, again legally, provided that their main job is to serve meals.

The surveying of young people **within** public houses gets further but might not elicit entirely truthful answers. Those conducting any survey presumably need the permission of a defensive publican. Some customers come back twice or appear more than twice in separate snug-bars and games' rooms. Looks alone do not count as several 13-year-old girls can pass for 16 or more, and the difference between a lad of 17 and one aged 20 is not always obvious. Better facts and figures might come from standing at a supermarket check-out point.

Many parents are as reluctant as publicans, shopkeepers and off-duty constables to reveal the true extent of their children's drinking habits. Nobody wants to be accused of not doing their job properly — or, in the case of some sales staff, doing their job too well!

So social scientists, politicians and teachers are left with that old standby: self-report, and thus depend on young people themselves to record their own consumption of alcohol. The disadvantages of self-report are:

- the temptation to boast
- the fear that someone in authority could identify the respondent
- haziness about which drinks are the strongest
- the limited intelligence of a few respondents
- the absence on the day of report of many regular drinkers
- defective memories
- consistent under-estimation of consumption (this applies to adults too)
- the time-span used: yesterday, last week, last month
- doubts or confusion about measures consumed, the size of glasses
- counting 'rounds' as drinks not actually purchased
- the possibility of ignoring top-ups at parties or buffets
- the context of the survey: in classroom, church, youth-club or the street. The context alters, or skews the response.

Nevertheless, self-report is the most reliable method of survey at the disposal of inquisitors, and self-report has produced many interesting — and consistent — results.

The Drinkwise survey for Drinkwise Day, 1989, asked adults when they remembered **starting to drink alcohol**. Half said they started before the age of 17, 15% before the age of 15, 2% before they were 12, 1% before they were 9. Berkshire teenagers reported 20% first drinking before the age of 10, balanced by 20% starting to drink after the age of 15, the other 3 in 5 sometime in between. The National Children's Bureau reached the figure of ¼ drinking by age 13 joined by another ½ by age 17.

Some teenagers have **never tasted alcohol**. *The Guardian* asked 1000 15 and 16 year olds and found only 2% had not had any alcoholic drink. A variant measure is one of young people **not currently drinking alcohol**. Here a Coventry survey found ¼ of boys aged 14 to 17 not drinking but this had fallen to 1 in 10 boys aged 18 to 21. In Chesterfield it was discovered that ⅓ of Grammer School sixth-formers were not drinking. An Oldham survey found 30% of young people under the age of 18 "not guilty" of underage drinking on licensed premises.

Many teenagers reportedly **drink once a week**. Coventry broadly found this number included ½ of boys and ⅓ of girls. The National Children's Bureau came up with the slightly lower figure of 30% of boys and 20% of girls. About 40% of boys aged 15 to 19 visit a public house once a week. Just over ½ of **all** young people aged 16 claim to drink once a week.

The **unit** or **standard drink** is a way of comparing like with like. One unit is roughly equivalent to ½ pint of beer (¼ pint of very strong beer), one glass of table-wine or one measure of whisky. The Office of Population Census and Surveys has come up with a definitive consumption figure for young people aged 16 or more: they were drinking an average of 9.4 units **during the past week**. The exact male figure was 14.5 units, the figure for females 4.8 units.

One quarter of Berkshire teenagers questioned said they only drink **on special occasions**. One fifth of 16 year-olds in another survey reported that they drank **once a month**. A Lothian survey in 1982 found that among 15 and 16 year-olds, 20% of boys and 14% of girls claimed to have drunk 8 units **on the last occasion** they drank.

That leads to the issue of **regular drinking**. One thorough Comprehensive School survey found ⅓ of girls drinking 2 units a week at the age of 11, when ½ of the boys were drinking 3 units a week. In that same school, ⅔ of pupils aged 15 were drinking 6 units every week.

The Lothian survey of 15 and 16-year-olds discovered 45% of boys and 32% of girls describing themselves as "regular drinkers".

Among young adults, P. Wilson's 1980 figure seems to hold good with young men aged 18 to 24 drinking an average of 28.1 units per week (compared with 20.3 units for all males) and young women aged 18 to 24 drinking 10.8 units per week (7.2 units for all women).

About one in 30 young people describe themselves as **problem drinkers** — almost certainly an underestimate as one in five of all young adults is a heavy drinker, and *Panorama* found ⅕ of all boys aged 15 drinking 20 or more units per week! The Office of Population Census and Surveys found that one in four men aged 18 to 24, and one in twelve women in the same age-band, were exceeding the recommended level of 21 units per week for men and 14 units per week for women.

A surprisingly large number of young people report that they **have been drunk** (in line with the bout drinking described in Chapter 4). *The Guardian* found ½ of all boys, (43% of all 16 year-olds), had been drunk at least once in the previous 6 month period; a quarter had had a hangover in the same period. 44% of Berkshire youth-club members said they had been "frequently intoxicated." Two authentic surveys found that ¾ of boys aged 15 had been drunk on at least one occasion, usually induced by consecutive consumption of 10 units or more. The National Children's Bureau discovered ¼ of boys aged 13 to 16 having suffered the severe after-effects of heavy drinking.

The Coventry survey pointed to **a cluster of symptoms** surrounding teenage drinking: loss of memory, solitary drinking, drinking alcohol before or instead of breakfast, becoming aggressive after drinking, and spending all one's money on alcohol. Between the ages of 14 and 17, one-quarter of boys and 15% of girls reported two or more "symptoms". In the older age-band 18-21, 42% of all respondents were experiencing two or more of these symptoms, becoming more psychologically dependent upon alcohol.

Turning to **the source of alcohol** 40% of young people under the age of 18 obtain alcohol from off-licences; 20% get their supply from the supermarket; 13% normally purchase their alcohol in a public house, leaving 9% taking it from home, and 9% drinking at a friend's home.

By the age of 17, 68% of males and 57% of females are consuming some of their alcohol in public houses. Just less than half of all 17-year olds are frequenting registered **clubs.** Very few surveys separate out **what drink** young people drink. Cider, shandy and tinned lager are obvious favourites and more available to young people. Under-age drinkers spend nearly £300 million per year on beer, which nevertheless has come down in popularity by 12½% in the past decade, as against a rise in the popularity of wine and cider: consumption up by 75% over ten years. It is estimated that twice as many 4th-form boys find beer-drinking congenial as do 4th-form girls. By that stage in their secondary school lives, one-quarter of boys and girls are drinking wine on a fairly regular basis.

A survey of teenagers **in France** found that alcohol consumption among 15 to 18 year-olds has doubled recently with ¼ of 12 to 18 year-olds drinking to excess. One in 5 French boys drink beer every week with 28% of those aged 16 to 17 drinking spirits at least once a week. One key finding in France was that there was twice the chance of young people **drinking daily** if their parents drank daily (26%, as against 13% of young people observing more moderate drinking).

International comparisons are never easy to make but reliable surveys indicate that, in the 14-17 age band, 70% of American, Canadian and West German young people are drinkers, 20% **heavy** drinkers.

Summary

Alarm surrounding the alcohol intake of young people led to great Victorian initiatives to introduce, if not to enforce, tougher licensing laws. Children continued however to carry alcohol home for their parents, sipping a little on the way. The Victorians also gave great impetus to the Temperance Movement whose momentum waned only from 1920 onwards.

Nobody can ever be sure **how much** modern young people actually drink, partly because accurate surveys depend on self-report which is often an under-reporting.

It would be fair to say, however, that young men drink more often than young women, and that they drink more alcohol on each occasion they go out drinking. There is evidence that girls are now closing the gap, drinking rather more wine in particular.

A large number of young people drink spasmodically or in bouts, with only a half of under-16-year-olds describing themselves as regular drinkers. One-tenth of all adults are acknowledged problem-drinkers and there might well now be that proportion of problem-drinkers among the young, with men aged 18 to 21 consuming very large quantities of alcohol (sometimes every day of every week).

The national consumption of alcohol doubled between 1950 and 1976, and it is probable that young people's drinking doubled in the same period, with a sharper upward turn since 1976.

Many local surveys have been attempted, particularly in schools. Results are difficult to compare because different questions are asked, and different (sometimes very wide) age-bands are used. New surveys need a large sample, if possible chosen at random. Anonymity needs to be guaranteed. The best questions to ask are very **specific,** eg: "How much alcohol did you consume yesterday?" "Did you have any alcohol last week?" or "How many times have you drunk an alcoholic beverage in a public house on a Saturday or a Sunday during the past month?"

CHAPTER TWO

Discovering the Impact

There's an amber hue in the sparking draught
And it brings to your eyes the light,
And your heart beats high when the bowl is quaffed —
Do you think of its cost to-night?
It will cost you wealth; it will cost you health;
It will rob you of peace and joy;
Will you drink? Will you drink? — at so great a price?
Will you drink? Will you drink, my boy?

from the Temperance Melodist, 1891

The impact of alcohol on anybody's life is always immediate, often extensive, sometimes complete. Factors which alter the impact of alcohol upon young people when compared with their elders include a lower tolerance threshold, a smaller income, less life experience, and a certain rashness or lack of inhibition — a factor which would characterise adolescence in any case.

Throughout this chapter, the intertwining of youthfulness and alcohol intake will be noted. But everybody is different, and extraneous factors like home background, schooling, peer-group relations, actual or suspected cruelty suffered, and genetic inheritance will impinge upon drinking behaviour and alter some of its consequences.

This is the appropriate point to introduce the useful concept of **the drinking career**. The word ''career'' has often been reserved for a series of jobs or examination results. This is a limitation. People have many careers, reflecting their simultaneous involvement in several enterprises of which drinking alcohol is one.

Young people do not typically follow just one of three simple drinking careers: light, moderate or serious. Instead they switch

9

over at different points. The young woman binger might become a regular lunchtime drinker when she gets her first salaried job, reverting to social drinking only during a first pregnancy, abstaining whilst her baby is young, later drinking to secure business contacts when she resumes paid employment.

That part of her drinking career is not the same as her brother's course. He begins as a cemetery drinker, for bravado, whilst only 13, but graduates to the public house by the age of 16½. His first (manual) job makes him a thirsty teatime drinker, but when his family responsibilities increase he changes to Sunday-lunch drinking only.

One portrait of a recognisable alcohol-soaked young offender emerged from Essex Probation Service during the Autumn of 1989. He is aged between 17 and 20, he drinks 15 pints of strong lager **a night**, and lives with his parents. He knows young men referred for Probation input who are consuming **between 100 and 120 pints a week** of extra strong beer. Sustaining such a habit costs him £7000 or more a year. Such a career is not actually very long. Death intervenes within two years.

No two drinking careers are identical but each career needs remembering and charting because each throws up valuable clues; each follows a pattern. Every drinking career is significant, whether it tails off, whether it degenerates into a lengthy illness, whether it remains entirely static, or whether it is suddenly terminated.

The Impact on Health

Whenever a harmful substance is even mentioned, people look for its effect on health. This is never more true than with cigarettes. So widespread has been the publicity given to the harmful effects of smoking, during the past 25 years, that smoking and health are inseparable considerations, and that despite powerful and unremitting tobacco product advertising at the same time. By a twist of irony, "teaser" advertisements, mentioning a clue (silk or colour) instead of a cigarette brand, lead to a situation where the only wording on the page is the Government health warning which is intended to **dissuade** purchasers.

As already stated in the Introduction, alcohol as a "social problem" has been medicalised. Doctors are the scientific advisers, the investigators, the pundits, the commentators, the agents of healing, the authors, and the prophets, all at the same time — as if health was everything, or at least, everything that mattered.

Alcohol undoubtedly does alter young people's health which then has a knock-on effect on other areas of their lives. Equally, other areas of their lives lead them to drink more, which then affects their health. Some pre-existing unhealthiness will actually be ameliorated by alcohol; some unhealthiness will be exacerbated by alcohol; a great deal of unhealthiness will run alongside regular drinking but will certainly not be improved by such consumption.

Nationally, 790,000 people have serious health problems associated with alcohol intake, about 2% of those over 16. Three million heavy drinkers display detectable biochemical abnormalities. One-third of premature deaths in middle-age are caused by alcohol (the biggest cause after cancer and heart disease) — but to protect surviving relatives, only one half of these deaths are recorded as due to excessive drinking.

Heavy drinkers have a mortality rate set at over twice that of the normal adult population. It is estimated that each year alcohol leads to 30,000 deaths in England and Wales alone. Included in that figure are the deaths of 500 young people following intoxication, 10% of all mortalities under the age of 25.

Alcohol kills 20 times the number killed by heroin and hard drugs put together, and although drinking before the age of 21 is unlikely to lead to death before the age of 25, life expectancy might well be shortened to 45. And death is merely the **worst** known consequence.

Mortality figures mask millions of unpleasant illnesses associated with alcohol, and the months of agony that may precede death. So alcohol-related hospital admissions need to be taken into account. Such admissions stand at one-fifth of all admissions, but in accident and emergency departments which treat more outpatients, that proportion becomes two-fifths of all patients.

After death and hospitalisation, another less quantifiable measure of alcohol's impact on health would be visits to the general practitioner. These visits increase with drinking, and very conservatively, alcohol-related surgery appointments cost the National Health Service an extra £2m per year.

Alcohol in drink tends to make water move out of the body cells and accumulate in the bloodstream. That accounts for the fact that alcohol rarely quenches thirst; also for the way alcohol's **instant** effects often differ from any long-term impact on healthiness.

In small quantities alcohol increases self-confidence, giving a higher level of energy, motivation, and loquacity. Worries recede. The body temporarily relaxes. But because alcohol is a depressant, not a stimulant, after a few drinks or a few hours, headaches,

The effects of alcohol are progressive. The more you drink, the worse are the effects. Drunkenness can cause loss of control and increase the likelihood of accidents. Alcohol is a poison and it can kill if taken in very large doses.

2 units
Accidents become more likely.

3 units
Cheerful and relaxed, but judgment is affected.

5 units
Risk of accident is 4 times greater than for 2 units. Illegal to drive.

10 units
Excitable, quarrelsome, slurred speech. 25 times greater accident risk than 2 units.

12 units
Staggering, memory loss, and double vision.

25 units
Blackout and collapse.

32 units
Death possible

(Reprinted by courtesy of Franklin Watts)

nausea, lack of concentration and dyspepsia follow. At night, there may be insomnia and the accompanying anxiety-state.

Alcohol is first absorbed by the mouth, then by the gullet, then by the stomach. Gradual body changes are soon mirrored in the face. The organ that eventually takes most of the strain of processing alcohol is the liver. When that is scarred and damaged, it changes its colour and its efficiency (cirrhosis of the liver). The liver can only process one standard drink each hour, and then not every hour.

If liver-damage is the best known indisposition caused by alcohol, other illnesses associated with heavy alcohol intake are hepatitis, gastritis, pancreatitis, cancers of the mouth, larynx and oesophagus, breast cancer, the irritable bowel syndrome and cardiac arrest. Additionally, drinkers face an increased risk of high blood-pressure, brain damage, even strokes.

Sometimes alcohol makes diabetes far worse, or it leads to acute vitamin deficiency. Depression can set in to become morbid or "endogenous" (as opposed to reactive depression) and many drinkers become suicidal. 40% of all overdoses follow, or include, alcohol consumption, and the risk of suicide might be 50 times greater for heavy drinkers when compared with the rest of the population. The whole body's chemistry is distorted by toxicity. If a young person is already taking a prescribed or even an over-the-counter drug, then it is likely that alcohol will react with that drug, causing an even greater bodily dysfunction.

When dreadful medical consequences are listed, human reaction is either: "it won't happen to me", or "I can take my drink". Drinkers tend to put off the evil day when the body will rebel or resign. That applies especially to young people who think in far shorter time-spans. Some young motorcyclists are particularly reckless, or else they are very competent riders, but fatalistic. "Eat, drink and be merry, for tomorrow we die."

Many health risks linked to alcohol can be substantially reduced by lessening the number of units of alcohol consumed each week; also by spreading units across the entire drinking week. Although there is certainly no "safe limit", doctors advise men not to exceed 20 units per week and women not to exceed 15 units per week, the equivalent of 7½ pints of ordinary beer or lager. The heavy youthful male drinker is so far adrift of this maximum recommended total that he might consume 40 units **a night** three nights each week.

Women can be more affected by alcohol than men because the

water content of their bodies — which might dilute alcohol — is 10% less as a proportion of body weight. Also women sometimes eat far less, and women have livers which are less resistant. A recent significant medical finding is that the linings of women's stomachs secrete different chemicals from those present in men's stomachs. These chemical reactions too make the absorption of alcohol more difficult.

Below 15 units per week for women in overall good health, and below 20 units per week for healthy men, alcohol intake is unlikely to cause any **long-term** health problems. At 16 to 24 units per week for women, 21 to 34 units for men, there is limited likelihood of long-term health risk **provided** drinking is spread throughout the week. Those women drinking 25 to 34 units weekly, and those men drinking 35 to 49 units **are likely** to `damage their health. Above that level: (35 units for women, 50 for men) physical and mental health **will** be damaged, and irretrievably.

The Impact on Weight

All young people are weight-conscious, and conscious of the weight of their friends and acquaintances. In this connection, both obesity and anorexia are alarming manifestations of a weight problem (as are the syndromes leading to, or resulting from, intermittent overeating).

Adolescents tend to laugh at their fathers' beer-paunches, or the bulbous red noses of their grandfathers. But lurking behind the comedy is a serious fear of flabbiness and unattractiveness. Not a few lads of 19 or 20 already have alcohol-distended bellies. One pint of beer commonly contains 180 calories, and even a low-alcohol beer contains 100 calories. Subsequent loss of appetite is no redress, particularly when the drinking night will often end with a greasy bag of fish and chips, or some fast-food concoction that the body has no time to process or reject before bedtime.

The Impact on Sexuality and Pregnancy

Alcohol, as will be seen later in this book, is heavily promoted for its supposedly beneficial effect on sexiness and sexual prowess. One teenager put it this way in GENERATION X: "If you go to a party and have a few beers, bed is the main thing you think about. Then you don't mind how rough the girl looks. Everyone looks beautiful when you've had a few drinks. Drink brings you down to the animal scale. Usually I don't sleep with a girl just for one night. That only happens when the girl and I have met while drinking."

That extract was taped before the AIDS scare. Since AIDS reached the headlines, politicians and doctors have been pointing to the danger of casual and promiscuous sexual intercourse. Such coition is far more likely after alcohol has been consumed, because inhibitions are reduced, and boys are unlikely to buy, to fit, and to keep hold of, a condom, and girls forget the pill.

Two other teenagers in GENERATION X throw a rather different light on the link between inebriation and sexual attraction: "I don't have much time for girls. I'm too busy drinking and playing darts;" and "If you're in a romantic mood and have a few beers, you say things you don't mean. Some girls take me seriously and expect me to rush up to them with a wedding ring."

Young women aged 15 to 20 are especially fertile and it is not improbable that one isolated act of intercourse, one temporary holiday romance, could lead to pregnancy. 4000 "Gymslip mothers" each year, under the age of 16, are no figment of the imagination. Mothers who do drink heavily during pregnancy risk foetal abnormalities and growth retardation, even still-births. Only very light drinking, less than 5 units per week, will be harmless to the unborn child.

Once pregnancy is discovered, many girls elect to have an abortion. They might be unprepared emotionally or scholastically for giving birth, or they may lack the support of reliable parents or a steady boyfriend. Or they might well remember — or wish to forget — the circumstances of the night they conceived, when they themselves were tipsy, or when their lovers, aggressors or abusers were drunk.

In 1987, 3765 girls aged 15 or under had a **legal** abortion. That amounted to 2.2% of all legal abortions performed in England and Wales. That year, 35,167 girls aged between 16 and 19, and 49,256 girls aged 20 to 24 had an abortion in a registered clinic or in hospital (20.5% and 28.6% of all abortions, respectively). A significant proportion of these unwanted pregnancies must have been alcohol-related.

The joker in the pack is the **impotence** associated with moderate or heavy drinking, particularly where the male is tired or stressed. The consumption of only 6 units in a day can impair male sexual performance. One health education poster mocks the failure of erection that follows an evening of drinking: "If you drink too much, there's one part that every beer can reach...." or a different poster: "A night of heavy drinking can make it impossible for you to make love... If you think your drinking isn't affecting you, have you ever wondered how it might be affecting your partner?''

Many heavy-drinking women have sexual difficulties too. They might find their responsiveness reduced, or they might develop menstrual problems such as cycle irregularities and amenorrhea.

Drunken and Disorderly Behaviour

The image of the "lager-lout" wending his way through the shopping centre with brightly coloured scarf stretched across his bronze chest, and the image of the drunken reveller on his way to a European football match, are familiar on our television screens. Unfortunately, this has created a mythology — the stuff of bold headlines in tabloid newspapers — which obscures the reality. There might well be a number of teenagers milling around, the worse for drink, but as with any behaviour, stealing, gambling or truanting, fact needs separating from fiction.

The published figures for drunken and disorderly behaviour will always be unreliable because:

- young people can be drunk without being disorderly
- young people can (less commonly) be disorderly without being drunk
- girls who drink and make a noise are excused on gender grounds
- those who are worse for drink need not be drunk
- disorderliness is often confined to the interior of public houses and is dealt with by publicans, with the help of their regulars
- drunken and disorderly behaviour within private houses is very rarely reported to the police
- young people who congregate after drinking could often be charged with rowdiness or causing an affray, but are simply moved on by the police
- local constabularies have vastly different ways of tackling, and reporting to crown prosecutors, drunkenness and disorderliness
- there is a certain pride in taking home a souvenir or a trophy after an evening's drinking. It could be a portable road-sign or a traffic cone or a workman's lamp, a beer-glass or a football fan's woolly hat, a poster or a door-handle. These are all technically "thefts", but are sometimes seen as mere high jinks.

Between 1950 and 1977, offences of drunkenness in England and Wales rose from 42,000 to 109,000. Between 1977 and 1984, whereas arrests of men rose by only 3%, arrests of women (the lager-loutesses?) increased by 22%. Convictions of under 18-year-olds have risen out of line with the conviction of adults. In 1964, just 1,850 teenage revellers were charged. The figure for 1976 was 4,805.

Interestingly, when there was evidence of a reduced intake of alcohol between 1979 and 1982, there were 16% fewer arrests for being drunk and disorderly. Between 1981 and 1982, when 10% less pure alcohol was consumed, 11% fewer young people were convicted of drunkenness, and 8% less were convicted of being drunk and disorderly.

Scotland has seen the greatest rise in the number of young people arrested for drunkenness: a rise of 90% in the 1980s. 40% of male Scots drink more than 8 units every day, compared with 27% of English men. Two-thirds of **all** young people arrested have been drinking in the previous 4 hours. Drink is a contributory factor in 78% of all assaults (more later) and 80% of all instances of breach of the peace. Criminal damage, a very teenage offence, has a very high correlation with drinking, and a staggering 93% of all arrests of young persons between the hours of 10pm and 2am follow intoxication.

The majority of those arrested for drunkenness are **not** actually chance partygoers, but are already confirmed drinkers. Those arrested for drunkenness draw attention to themselves by begging, by urinating in a public place, by sleeping rough, or by intentionally throwing a stone through the window of some large shop or police station. 60% of young people arrested for drunkenness are also homeless. Half have had no contact with parents or siblings for over a year. 40% are currently unemployed.

Arrests for drunkenness under the age of 21 used to be a small minority: 10%. That proportion now stands at 25%. Even so, arrests for drunkenness of men aged 49 to 56 are 25 times greater than for boys aged 14 to 16, and 10 times greater than for young men aged 17 to 20.

Crowd Problems

Mass crowd behaviour is a different phenomenon from the behaviour of couples or groups. Crowds nurture a mood or an atmosphere that is very distinctive. The whole is indeed more than the sum of the parts. Usually, crowds are cheerful, bustling, inquisitive and noisy. Occasionally, crowds swing unpredictably after only a minor scuffle or an altercation in their midst. Rumour spreads quickly in a crowd. Bodies jostle and rub against each other in a way that overcomes an insistence on room, and the reticence of most participants.

The impact of drink on crowds is not necessarily the same as drunkenness, or even disorderly intent. When a crowd gathers outside a public house it may number a hundred. Great crowds at festivals and sporting events could be made up of **50,000** restless individuals. Royal weddings, walkabouts and air displays attract large crowds. Marches of protest and demonstrations would at least keep crowds moving, if only police did not keep blocking the route or shutting side-streets.

Young people are keener to join marches because they have more idealism and optimism than most of their elders. Also a march is a fascinating occasion with a ready-made adversary which is not necessarily Apartheid, the Arms Race or Commercial Whaling (although young people's passion and environmental concern is usually genuine). Student and campus demonstrations by their very nature attract almost entirely under-25 year olds.

Many people in a crowd have already drunk alcohol, if only with their packed lunches, or else they have obtained alcohol for later on. If a march is friendly, alcohol is both expected and excused. If a big race or grand-prix has just ended, alcohol is an ostentatious part of victory. The same applies to great state occasions except for sombre funerals. Newspapers coyly refer to "a party spirit".

Sometimes the police sense that they are outnumbered and that there is a likelihood of "ugly scenes". If a true riot is on the cards, reinforcements are drafted in, armed with batons, CS gas, flimsy plastic shields and rubber bullets. Alcohol inflames just that flash-point, or clash-point, when everybody panics and tempers are frayed.

Sadly it is often in the police's interest to assert that most secondary pickets, most marchers, most members of ethnic minorities, most devoted football supporters, and most of those lying down in front of Cruise missiles, are drunk, or have been drinking. The demise of the Notting Hill Carnival has been blamed on drink and drugs — for they are safer culprits than racism and run-down housing.

The most famous recent crowd trouble occurred in and around the Hillsborough football stadium in Sheffield on the occasion of the 1989 F.A. Cup semi-final between Nottingham Forest and Liverpool. Many spurious accounts appeared in the newspapers after the ensuing disaster: stories that local pubs had run dry, that surviving fans had punched rescuers and had looted the pockets of the dead. Supt. Brian Mole told the Taylor Inquiry that the fans had stayed in public houses till just before kick-off: "We (the police) try to discourage the use of drink, and because they (the fans) realise this, those intent on finding drink must look for other avenues, pubs further afield.'' Later in 1989 some of the wilder allegations in the press were retracted.

Instances of Violence

Any discussion of drunken and disorderly behaviour (unhelpfully the butt of music-hall jokes) or any following of crowds leads naturally to the weightier question of violence: violence in and around public houses, street violence, violence outside nightclubs and fast-food shops, violence in market squares or down lonely alleys.

A Parole Board survey found that in more than 80% of cases of unpremeditated violent crime, including murder, drink had been a factor. 40% of all members of Alcoholics Anonymous report that they have been in a serious fight. In Scotland, 92% of all violent crime follows drink. One-sixth of Berkshire teenagers surveyed reported being in a serious fight, with nearly all the sample having witnessed one.

In an evening fight both the aggressor and the victim will probably have been drinking. Hospital casualty departments report these injuries as some of the more common results of fighting:

heads cut open/teeth knocked out/broken arms and legs/ stabbing wounds to the back/slashed cheeks/crushed abdomens/ concussion/deep cuts in and around the shoulders/broken ribs/ cauliflower ears/embedded broken glass/extensive bruising around the eyes/severed testicles.

As if this were not enough, several injuries, especially internal damage, are far more difficult to detect **because** the patient has been drinking. It only then takes the appearance of a policeman, a long wait in casualty, the re-entry of the assailant, the attentions of an immigrant doctor, or some diagnostic questioning — and the injured person starts a fight **with medical staff.**

Excluding admissions after road-traffic accidents, nearly two out of every three male admissions to Accident and Emergency departments had drunk six pints of beer or more. At one infirmary, 62% of **all** those treated for head injuries were discovered with alcohol in their bloodstreams. The mean blood/alcohol level of those who had drunk and then sustained severe injury was 193mg: 2½ times the level for driving within the law.

When Jon Shepherd did a survey of the victims of assault, he found that 75% of them had been drinking. 50% had consumed

5 units: 2½ pints of beer or its equivalent. The average consumption of male victims was 10 units, of female victims — 6 units. One of the saddest features in the lives of wives and girlfriends who suffer male violence is their reluctance to report their aggressors to the police, perhaps out of misplaced loyalty, or resulting from an assurance that he "will never do it again". Frequently, battered women are told that they provoked their menfolk's drunken outburst.

After rapes (sometimes rapes within marriage) and horrific sexual attacks following drink, there is also an under-reporting of injury **to** the aggressor, injury not caused by the victim or his protectors. Hand injuries follow a common pattern. The knuckle is squashed and the back of the hand shows tooth-marks. Inside the hand, the tendons are torn with resultant loss of use in some of the fingers (hammer fingers). Injuries to the thumb are particularly serious because in the thumb rests half the hand's efficiency. A smashed hand must be kept in one position for up to 6 weeks. Torn tendons often only have one chance to heal after lesion.

Some prominence has been given to potentially violent mobs of young people gathering in quiet country towns on a Saturday night looking for trouble. This has been defined as a problem of "Thatcher's children", or "the champagne louts", of the prosperous South-East, although the phenomenon was first evident in the city of Lincoln early one New Year's Day a few years back. Like all good stories, recurrences are much sought after by journalists until the subject is truly out of the headlines.

In June 1988, Brian Hayes, Chief Constable of Surrey, collated factors relating to 250 incidents of serious disorder which came to his notice during 1987. 55% of these incidents were sparked off in small towns and villages. Street fights accounted for 62% of the incidents, with a further 20% happening on licensed premises. If one looks to a medium-sized provincial city like Nottingham, one can discover 200 pubs, bars and night-clubs inside 1 square mile. On a weekend evening these attract an average of 200 young spenders each, older boys and girls from all over South Nottinghamshire. Some customers are highly mobile **between** establishments, taking their unresolved fueds with them. These extra 40,000 drinkers and hangers-on pose a special challenge to Nottingham police patrols.

One Home Office Research report released in 1989 traced drunken posses of young people not to rural retreats but to quite large market and industrial "satellite" towns near to London, but not exactly part of the metropolitan conurbation. Researchers compared towns like Woking, Guildford, Sudbury and Gravesend. Local licence restrictions and the number of nightspots did have a direct bearing on hostile crowd behaviour, but the anecdotal evidence pointing to "problem towns" like Reading could not be substantiated. One town's figures were much like another's. The North did not tend to have the same Saturday-night fever, but so-called lager louts resort to violence wherever they imagine they have been pushed too far, or accused unjustly.

The Home Office team painted a picture of how an incident could develop: "Youths, well tanked up, are ejected onto the streets, sometimes carrying cans of beer. They wander down to local takeaways and then stand about watching the talent, talking, waiting, and hoping to meet someone or for something to happen. Inevitably some of the lads, many of whom are over-excited, or who have drunk too much... stumble against each other or insults are passed. The police are called. Perhaps the whole incident calms down and the lads disappear home. Perhaps it escalates..."

I had a recent, fortunately trivial, experience of the **potential** for escalation. I was standing at a crowded bar waiting to order some food. When the barman caught my eye and asked for my order I blurted out: "One steak and kidney..." whereupon the chap in front protested to the barman: "Eh, I was here first." I retaliated: "I **did** wait to be **asked** for my order." When that provoked no response I sighed heavily and was told: "All right. Cool it!" I was just about to underline my point by saying: "I am not in the habit of pushing in..." when I remembered that my self-righteousness could easily come across as an accusation that **he** had pushed in.

Some jokes are taken more seriously than intended by drinkers. Some sideways glances are mistaken for unfaithfulness. Some old grievances are resurrected during a tense Saturday evening. Some playful fights are not mutually understood as such. Some innocent bystanders cannot maintain their rôle as impartial witnesses. Ironically, there is some prestige and notoriety to be gained by being arrested. In the heat of battle, arrest is both a face-saver and a place of safety!

Drink-Driving

Society is still surprisingly tolerant towards drunken car drivers — more than they would be towards drunken bus drivers, drunken taxi drivers, drunken train drivers or the drunken pilots of aeroplanes. Not a few passengers — especially teenage passengers needing to get home after a night out — consent to be driven by drivers very much under the influence of drink.

Perhaps a misplaced concern for civil liberties, and a worship of the automobile, have softened people's alertness over such crimes committed at close quarters. It took many years to persuade Parliament to pass the 1967 Road Traffic Act which led to the introduction of the breathalyser, and which fixed the permitted blood/alcohol limit at 80mg (approximately the equivalent of 2½ pints of lager). Officials at the Ministry of Transport argued for a limit of 50mg and motoring organisations and other road groups argued for 100mg. so Barbara Castle (the Minister of Transport) arbitrarily settled for 80mg.

Since then, there have been repeated attempts to toughen up the law by lowering the limit, by increasing penalties for those caught, by introducing random breath-testing or by confiscating vehicles pending a very early court hearing. Yet the 1967 Act stands, only tinkered with, **and relaxed**, by an accumulation of case law, and by a token move recently to restrict insurance policies taken out by drinking drivers. At times, local police have had to interpret the law more broadly and firmly than the Home Office first suggested: by waiting near public houses, by stopping motorists to check tyres and tax-discs, by locking up offenders overnight, and by intensifying operations around Christmas. This has been dubbed: "harassment". In Australia, the drinking driver stands a one in three chance of random arrest. In Britain that chance is reduced to one in 250 drinking drivers. One in 60 evening motorists **would** have been over the limit if they had been stopped in their tracks.

Teenage drinkers behind the wheel will be far more of a menace than older drivers who have been drinking, and that is frightening when one considers how some middle-aged company car drivers treat other motorists in the fast lane, or cyclists and pedestrians on country lanes. Special teenage factors are:

- many teenagers ride motorcycles which are already involved in a disproportionate number of crashes resulting in injury or death

- a powerful motorcycle is harnessed to far more horsepower than is needed to propel its weight
- several teenage motorists stopped by the police have stolen the vehicle in which they are travelling
- when driving a stolen vehicle, they have far more need to avoid those they think are in hot pursuit
- "joy-riders" do not generally fear damaging the paintwork or the shells of their stolen vehicles, so they take more risks
- "joy-riding" has less stigma than other forms of theft and robbery, so penalties are generally light, even for multiple offences. the euphemism does not help; "TWOC" — taking without owner's consent — is not a much better term
- legitimate teenage drivers are far more likely than other motorists to be heading to or from a dance or a party
- legitimate teenage drivers are also far more likely to be carrying admiring or daredevil passengers (often themselves the worse for drink)
- because they have limited experience on the road, young drivers are more likely to panic when faced with a sudden hazard like cones, a road-block, an obscure junction, rapid lights, or a disabled couple crossing the road just ahead
- teenagers use speed and erratic road discipline to impress their friends and to prove their newly-acquired road-handling skills.

Any intake of alcohol affects driving skill, and not for the better. As little as one pint of beer can increase driver-error by 40% and reduce peripheral vision by 10%. Two pints of beer can seriously lengthen reaction-time: the time between seeing a hazard and using the information by braking or swerving. When travelling at 40mph, one-tenth of a second can keep a car travelling a further six feet. Slow reactions cause many shunting accidents. When a queue of traffic forms quickly, the last car to show its brake-lights will be two or three seconds behind the first driver who was held up.

Manchester Corporation once tested its drivers on private land after they had drunk some alcohol. Tiny amounts of alcohol led to diminished performance and shakier vehicle control. Drivers taking part in the experiment recalled what they **would** do in certain situations, which was different from what they actually **did**. A few drivers cheerfully tried to steer their 8-foot wide buses between cones spaced exactly 8 feet apart! With a blood/alcohol level of under 10mg, some wobbling across the road was evident. A level of only ½ the maximum permitted to car-drivers made an extraordinary difference to normally competent bus drivers.

Using a set of ordinary drivers at an accident black-spot as a control, it can be shown that at 80mg there is twice the chance of being involved in a moving traffic accident. 150mg produces **ten** times the risk; 200mg produces 20 times the risk. The use of daylight at the black-spot banishes the argument that a higher proportion of night-time drivers have been drinking in any case. No wonder insurance companies find that drink-drivers are an almost uninsurable risk, despite accidents being blamed on the build-up of **other** factors. Police can accurately predict what crashes will happen where and when.

One study into 2,000 recent road accidents found that there had been some drink-driving in 25% of them, with alcohol as the major contributing factor in 9%. In Scotland 18 people are arrested for drink-driving offences for every 10 arrested in England and Wales. (That trend runs through all statistics about the prevalence of drinking in Scotland.) Overall, drink-driving offences doubled between 1970 and 1980, and drink-driving costs society a minimum of £100m. a year.

As with victims of violence, the **victims** of drink-driving offences are often themselves over the legal limit. One-third of all dead drivers have a blood/alcohol level above 80mg.%, and over half of dead pedestrians at night fall into that category. On a **Saturday** night, 71% of all drivers who die between 10pm and 4am (on the Sunday morning) are also over the limit.

Road accidents after drinking are the biggest single cause of death in all young men. Half of all deaths to people under the age of 25 are road casualties. Young women are now drinking more. They are also driving more. Those frail jokes about slow women drivers nervously and passively edging their way out on to Britain's busy roads no longer apply. Young women, particularly on company business, are beginning to show the same driving behaviour as their male counterparts. Manufacturers of fast hatchbacks, Minis, and "special editions" are targetting young women, with lucrative results. The number of women actually arrested for drinking and driving trebled between 1974 and 1984.

Other Accidents

One third of all home accidents are alcohol related. The fine judgment needed to fix some shelves, to wash some high windows, or to rewire an appliance is affected by quite a small dose of alcohol.

Even house fires are often drink-related. Parents take risks with discarded cigarette ends and with open fires, or else they go down to a public house without arranging for proper babysitters. Arsonists have often been drinking too.

There is a definite correlation between drinking and death by drowning. A third of all young men and women who drown are discovered to have drunk alcohol beforehand.

The link between drinking and industrial accidents is less easy to detect because the **immediate** cause of those accidents is put down to something falling or collapsing, mechanical failure, some traction unit running out of control, or some interruption of the normal industrial process.

All these accidents — the coincidence of several circumstances in a moment or two of destruction — are far more likely to happen when the operative or his supervisor have been drinking. Scaffolders and crane-drivers are especially at risk. It is safe to say that in over 40% of industrial accidents, drink is one contributory factor; and significantly more accidents happen at the beginning of shifts, particularly the 2pm and the 10pm shifts.

Young workers will already have less experience and less caution on the shop floor, coping with new machinery, and climbing to higher heights. Their Y.T.S. or Employment Training Scheme will involve one supervisor shared between several apprentices each one of whom might be in high spirits and at an early peak in his drinking career.

Loss of Job

It is estimated that between 8 and 14 million working days are lost each year because of alcohol. That might cost £600m. per year in lost production alone. Many young people undoubtedly lose their jobs through drinking, although this again may not show up on their certificates of dismissal.

Some young workers turn up to work with drink on their breath; more drink at lunchtime; some secretly drink **during** work hours, more so if they are in the catering trade. Dismissal may nominally be for the poor timekeeping, for the avoidable accident, for the clash with colleagues, for the low productivity, for the loss of detail in work finished-matters all directly proportionate to drinking behaviour. 52% of dismissed workers blame drink. 43% of workers questioned say that drink led to an accident at work.

The "hangover" naturally increases absenteeism. Monday mornings are bad for hangovers. If a person has 8 standard drinks in quick succession, his body will require at least 8 hours to overcome the effects. Dehydration is one factor in any hangover. Water moves out of body cells into the bloodstream. Another factor in hangovers is the artificial additives contained in certain alcoholic beverages to give them their colour, flavour, smell and taste. Red wine, port, and brandy have most additives and lead to the worst hangovers. Gin, vodka and white wine contain fewer additives.

There is a heavy onus on firms and on local government employers not to be seen to be sacking employees for their drink problems. Drink may be an essential ingredient of the day's work: for entertaining customers, for doing deals, for getting a good newspaper story, or for serving drinking customers. Managers might themselves have a drink problem, and might not be setting the best example to their subordinates. Also there is a certain taboo around alcohol as a potential menace, and the families of employees have to be protected. Far kinder to send someone home for being "not really up to the job".

Loss of Money

Young people spend a vast proportion of their disposable incomes on alcohol. They are tempted to do so because:

- alcohol retains its position as supreme in teenage leisure
- alcohol consumption is a relatively cheap evening's entertainment, more so summer-time out-sales
- alcohol prices have lagged behind the level of inflation
- some young people have relatively high earnings
- parents are often ready not to charge a full commercial rate for board, or for board and lodgings
- conversely, parents often **lend** money to teenagers and young adults in the family
- grandparents often open savings accounts or leave legacies for their grandchildren
- casual earnings (very low earnings) are tolerated most by young people
- teenagers have fewer family responsibilities
- there is a supposition that "they deserve a good time when they're young"
- rounds turn out more expensive than buying for self alone
- some young people can buy friendship with alcohol.

Because young people are involved in a disproportionate number of shoplifting offences and burglaries, part of their disposable income spent on drink is probably stolen. Other young people may **sell** stolen goods, or "find" money at home.

Young people too young **legally** to drink in public houses nevertheless spend at least £300m. per year in public houses. *Panorama* in 1987 came up with an average disposable weekly income for all 15 to 17 year olds of £21.07. Those who drank alcohol at all spent £10, just under half their incomes, on drink. One typical girl — a part-time earner — said on *Panorama* that she got through 12 gins a night at weekends, and that nearly all her wage went on alcohol.

One young person in every 20 spends nothing on alcohol; 10% spend between £5 and £10 per week, and 25% of young people spend between £3 and £5. In 1961 it would have taken the average male manual worker 23 minutes to earn enough for one pint of beer. By 1981, he needed to work for only 12 minutes. Similarly the bottle of whisky that used to absorb 6 hours' labour, by 1981 cost the product of a mere 2 hours' labour. Of all drinkers, men aged between 18 and 24 drink most and thus spend most on alcohol: more than clothes or hobbies or stocking up a bottom drawer, more than even the smoking and gambling that so often accompanies drinking, more too than travelling to away matches.

That is a startling conclusion when it is remembered that young people are spending more than ever on fashion and clothes. The average young woman shops for clothes three times each month and spends between £20 and £50 monthly on her attire. Also, more young people own and run some means of private transport — which is an obvious candidate to displace alcohol in the spending league. One memorable health education poster on the subject of smoking showed a smouldering cigarette gradually burning away some one-pound notes. The equivalent nowadays would be a basket of £5 notes drenched in alcohol beyond any hope of retrieval.

Summary

The impact on young people's lives resulting from their steady or unsteady drinking careers is as diverse as all their activities, hobbies and relationships. This chapter has simply touched on a few of the more obvious consequences of teenage drinking.

Each reverberation is initially stark: death through liver failure, hospitalisation, the terrible car-crash, loss of job, drowning, arrest, the big fight in the beer garden, the crowd stampede, the empty wallet. And it is right to draw attention to these extremes.

Certainly, Victorian moralists never lacked melodrama in spelling out the direst consequences of intoxication.

However, lesser results **also** matter, the results that do not reach any headlines: the employer's warning, the half-empty wallet, the police caution, the dropped knife, the pair of young men forcibly separated by their friends, the broken engagement, parents waiting up anxiously, the mild hangover, the missed promotion, the near-miss, the meandering car, the sudden braking, minor cuts and bruises, the tummy upset and the failed examination.

For it is not only **paid** work that suffers from a hangover. One schoolday in every 30 lost through truancy is the result of drinking. Much more schoolwork in class deteriorates. It is said that all the ingredients of the 1989 Hillsborough Disaster could have happened one year beforehand, with the same match in the same ground between the same teams. Many supporters in the **1988** crowd were seriously concerned, frightened at the overcrowding and the crowd's volatility. But they had no way of sounding a warning. Similarly, doctors, parents and teachers who presently observe trouble resulting from young people's drinking have no way of sounding a warning without being cast in the role of killjoys who are alarmist and out-of-touch.

Even after adding up all that is negative in alcohol's balance-sheet, it must still be stressed that very few happenings are **direct** cause-and-result. Alcohol is still very much a hidden agent, a hidden force, a hidden menace.

CHAPTER THREE

Discovering the Context

The drinking den of gilded shame
For you its doors will open wide
To rob you of your honest name
And take away your manly pride;
But ere the sparkling wine you drink,
To lead your soul astray,
Just for a moment stop and think:
"Oh, what would mother say?"
"Oh, what would mother say?"
If she but saw me doing this —
"Oh, what would mother say?"

from the Temperance Melodist, 1891

The drinking venue, the drinking habitat, the drinking milieu, the drinking resort — all have an unusual importance for young people wanting to drink and to socialise, to drink and not to socialise, or to socialise but not to drink.

The place **of** drinking soon becomes the place **to** drink. A conscious selection is made of just where to drink, more conscious than where to engage in other teenage activities like grazing, cycling, jousting, smoking, walking, talking, watching television, or standin' doin' nothin'.

British young people do not grow up in the Mediterranean where grapes are routinely gathered and fermented, and where wine-lakes never run dry. Nor is beer served with the school dinner. Because for many younger teenagers drinking alcohol is still **officially** frowned upon, the right place to drink is not obvious straightaway.

The nearest equivalent is teenage courting and lovemaking.

Although serious friendships with the opposite sex are formed more in private than the start of a drinking career, **the place** to court is carefully chosen, its secrecy closely guarded. Teenagers might more readily make love or sip wine in a house where no adults are wandering about downstairs. However, if such a house is not available, or if siblings are prying, a cold cemetery, a damp park-bench or the cramped back-seat of a car are infinitely preferable.

Girls are thrown into confusion when they find themselves courting at the same time as their mothers and step-mothers. Likewise, boys are thrown into confusion when they find their quiet drink interrupted by father coming in with **his** cronies to prop up the same bar!

First Place: The Home

Notwithstanding the desire for privacy, maybe **because** of that desire, the home remains a popular venue for drinking. Most young people report that they had their very first sip of alcohol within the home, with Sunday Dinner, with Christmas Dinner, or because an elder sister had acquired a bottle. Some Dads self-consciously draw their boys aside on the 14th birthday that is supposed to mark a transition into adulthood so that their sons can share that first can of lager.

Certainly it is in the home where every child will carefully observe, and monitor, a parent's pattern of alcohol consumption or abstinence from alcohol. Every poll, study or investigation shows young people copying their parents, following their lead. Just as two chain-smoking parents are unlikely to bring up a non-smoking youngster, so two moderate drinkers are unlikely to give birth to a teetotal child.

Many parents do not frown at their teenage children drinking within the home. That is because:

- the parents might be drinking at the same time
- the parents might have sent their child out to buy ale
- the young person might be sharing **his own** alcohol with parents
- everybody might be testing home-brew
- the young person might only be having a token drink, not displaying his full drinking repertoire
- it might be the custom for everyone to drink round a hired video, or a favourite TV programme
- the young person might be an earner in her own right
- it might be a family celebration

- company might have come
- parents might be anxious to avoid another damaging confrontation
- the young person might have gained equality through age: 13, 15, 17, 19 or 21.

As already hinted, covert drinking at home begins when parents go out — perhaps to their local! Then a friend on his own brings round a six-pack, or the cocktail cabinet is raided. Some young people beat their parents' ingenuity marking how far a bottle is down — by filling up the shortfall with water! One or two homes have a complete bar fitted in the corner of the living-room to mirror the local public-house, a giant bottle of whisky upturned and fixed to the wall with a rawlplug. Few drinks' cabinets are locked. Few hidey-holes are completely unknown. Few supermarket trolleys are ·emptied to the count. A teenager does not have to be very clever to obtain her parents' alcohol. The curtains do not even have to be drawn.

Discarding the evidence is not such a problem as discarding a tampon or a condom or a "girlie" magazine. The dustbin might already be full to the brim with empty cans and unreturned bottles.

Since the advent of cable and satellite television this side of the Atlantic, parents have been offered devices for restricting their children's viewing whilst children are in the house unsupervised. Such master-switches have not sold well. Children have got the message implicitly and explicitly that they can view what they want when they want. Similarly, they can **drink** much of what they want when they want. Very few parents wish to enforce a double standard. Derek Rutherford, Director of the Institute of Alcohol Studies, has put it this way: "Parents throw up their hands in despair if their child is caught smoking marujuana but sigh with relief if they have only been raiding the cocktail cabinet." Indeed, a survey of 35,000 children conducted by the Schools Health Education Unit revealed that one in four boys and one in five girls are **given** alcohol regularly within their homes. If parents are ever confronted with their complicity, their first reaction is usually one of anger. They think they are being blamed for being irresponsible.

Second Place: The Street

Street drinking is problematic, partly because the traditional High Street is hardly what is meant: more the side street; more the alley or the twitchel; more the courtyard outside the football ground or the amusement arcade; more the rabbit-warren-like passages in a modern council house estate; more the "dead-storey" of a multi-storey block of flats where the garbage bins are stored; more the churchyard or the corner of the school playing-field.

If the High Street **is** the uppermost image, one imagines a dissolute tramp, hip-flask on hairy chest, prostrate on a wooden bench in front of a wooden flower-tub, all his belongings in that large red spotted handkerchief; or one pictures a wan and wafer-thin woman slumped outside Woolworths, at first only visible through her long thick matted hair.

Drinking outdoors in public view is still legal, although in 1988 an amendment to an Act of Parliament paved the way for individual councils to encode a model by-law prohibiting the consumption of alcohol in the street. Coventry is one city where this restriction will be tested as a social experiment. Even in Coventry it is not envisaged that the police will arrest every family having a picnic by the lakeside, nor will they necessarily push back public house overspill on a hot Summer evening.

Undoubtedly, it is the ready sale of alcohol in off-licences, garages, video-shops and supermarkets at greatly reduced prices that has encouraged young people to drink on the curb-edge or in the great outdoors. Tipping up a brightly-coloured tin of lager does not look very different from tipping up a tin of the ubiquitous Coca-Cola. Slight class differences emerge, as with the eating of fish-and-chips. It is very **down-market** to eat and drink on the pavement. Posh people go into cafés, or whisk their curries back (in the car) to dining-room tables. The beer-garden, and the picnic out of wicker basket, are exceptions to this class differential.

Third Place: The Party

To any child growing up in the 1950s, the image of a party was a series of innocent games and charades performed beneath funny crêpe fancy-hats and decorations. At a certain point in the proceedings, the plonking on the piano ceased and the children leapt to take their fill of a Beano-like feast of jellies, multi-coloured blanc-manges, trifles, fairy-buns, sausage rolls, salmon and egg sandwiches, and sausages on sticks.

That is a far cry from the adult party of nowadays, the young adult party, or even the contemporary children's birthday party — with its stereo amplifiers blaring, its steaming hamburgers straight out of McDonald's, and its flickering spotlights. Parties at **all** levels have become more sophisticated, more frenetic, and more soaked in alcohol. Many parties have done away with food altogether. The bar is the focus of partygoers' attention with the distant hope of some roast-chicken flavoured crisps, and a pinch of peanuts.

Teenage parties have a reputation all of their own. Here are four examples:

1) The Acid House Party

This takes place in a deserted mill or barn in an obscure location. One of two days before the event, tickets are purchased in the city centre. On the back of each ticket are 2 or 3 phone numbers to be rung on the actual night to gain directions to the exact venue. This Acid party might not start until 1am on a Saturday or a Sunday morning; it will then last till 5 or 6am. Drinking will be fairly heavy. Drugs, including CRACK — a derivative of Cocaine — might be on sale. Police will almost certainly raid the party after being rung up by shocked country bumpkins. Needlessly, the parties have already advertised themselves with pop music loud enough to wake the slumbering cows and to send grazing ponies into a stampede. The question remains — which comes first: the bad publicity or the underground party?

2) The Undergraduate Party

This type of party is held in the common room of a hall of residence or in the dining room of the Students' Union. Partygoers are expected to bring their own drinks. Ostensibly, the party celebrates Doug's successful driving test or Debbie's 21st, but any excuse will do. Students will generally be well-dressed and spend more time chatting than dancing to the strains of a semi-professional group hired for the evening in their 'P' registered Transit van. Party ends at midnight.

3) The Open-Door House-Party

This party commonly takes place in the home of one young person whose parents are away on holiday, or who have fled. Gatecrashers are not welcome, but gatecrashers are inevitable. A great deal of alcohol is purchased by both the host and her guests, and new supplies are brought in for later on. Casual sexual liaisons develop in different parts of the dimly-lit house, and not too much care is taken of any antique furniture or Capo di Monte china left exposed. Again, music wakes the neighbours who then threaten to call the police. A few amphetemines and purple-hearts may be passed round, and cannabis might be smoked openly. With any luck, the house will empty at 3am — but anytime after 11.30pm, one or two anxious parents can be seen drawing up outside to collect their love-bitten offspring.

4) The Closed-Door House-Party
This party will celebrate an 18th birthday, the end of GCSE Exams or a home-coming from abroad. The guest-list of between 12 and 22 will be carefully chosen. This time, guests, and **their** guests, will be closely watched, and even turned out if they appear disruptive. Mum and Dad may wisely decide to stay around, barricaded in their upstairs bedroom, desperately trying to concentrate on the inferior picture flickering across the 13″ screen of their black-and-white portable TV. At such a protected party alcohol will flow less freely: perhaps a few Babychams, three large flagons of cider, and some cans of shandy. The odd jug of orange juice or apple juice might make its appearance. Also food will be re-introduced, not much food or very elaborate, but plenty of salty snacks, cheese cobs and chocolate biscuits. At the end of the evening as midnight approaches, the homely record-player will be switched off, and borrowed singles will be returned to their owners. No flashing lights. No bare-boards. No heavy petting. The best sort of party for home-centred young people daring to spread their wings just a little.

Other teenage parties take place at schools, youth clubs, night-clubs and in Sunday School rooms. Here the **ownership** of the properties alters the content and direction of the parties. Local authority and chapel caretakers are not the most broad-minded of officials.

Alcohol matters at teenage parties simply because much teenage drinking is still bout or binge-drinking: not very often but in fairly large quantities. The Home Office Research Unit in 1989 discovered that one third of their Guildford sample on a Saturday night had drunk more than 4 pints of beer, or the equivalent. The same team revealed that one-tenth of young men questioned (under the age of 24) had drunk over **eight** pints on a Saturday night. Alcohol also matters because teenage parties would be boisterous, wild and sexy even without the drink on tap — so there is endless potential for trouble.

Some teenagers save up all their pocket-money for one rotating party each fortnight, one knees-up guaranteed to knock everyone backwards. Thus, they will not have a **gradual** introduction to intoxication, and the apprenticeship to many teenage drinking careers will be foreshortened. Parties are exciting because they are so unpredictable. Police, neighbours and returning parents banging on the door only add to the excitement, and the loss of respectability. At the same time, adults-only parties rarely invite **young** teenagers under 17. Even the more sedate and controlled parties offer an endless opportunity for young people, in anonymity, and without inhibition, to explore new experiences, and to forget dull daily routines. Forming new relationships is hard work.

Fourth Place: The Special Occasion

Young people enjoy most special occasions except toddlers' parties, and they drink because drink has become synonymous with celebration. As noted already, young revellers congregate at big matches, big marches, at each other's comings-of-age, and at "house-warmings" that certainly live up to their name. Adulthood comes at the **legal** start to a drinking career. Celebrating with something stronger than fizzy is a mark of adulthood, and adult festivities.

Many young people report that they had their first proper drinks at a Wedding Reception. Some receptions in church halls are "dry" because the hall is covenanted not to sell or stock alcohol. At many other receptions, alcohol is limited to a glass of sherry on entry, a glass of wine with the meal, and champagne with the toasts. However, some receptions have an open or free bar, or have waitresses circulating with never-ending refills. If a reception is split into two parts: formal meal and evening disco, then the evening disco might have a free bar. Merry young adults stand round waiting for their first dance with the bride.

Day trips are that other special occasion dripping with alcohol. Some coaches arrive at horse-races, regattas and funfares — but not now at football matches — with boots stacked with crates of beer. Other working-men's outings stock up for the journey home. The whole purpose of some day-trips to Channel ports is to stock up with alcohol at (supposedly) cheaper prices. Not a few coaches on their way back from Ostend or Dover have had to be stopped and emptied by police because liquor is taking them above their weight limit. Many picnics and fishing-trips also rely on drink, as do the great pop festivals attracting teenagers from hundreds of miles away.

Fifth Place: On Holiday

Mention needs to be made of holiday drinking as a special category. It was a brief series of early Sunday evening "interlude" programmes back in 1983: *"That's the Limit"*, that first alerted me to the peculiar problems associated with holiday drinking. Since then, the issue has been more widely debated in case English men (and women) are failing as the nation's ambassadors overseas.

Young people who go abroad do so either in couples, or in small groups, unless they are still tied to their parents' apron strings. Younger holidaymakers are unlikely to stay in ordinary 3-star hotels or in quiet mountain resorts. Instead they congregate in fun resorts like Ibiza, Playa de Palma (Majorca), Aghios Nikolaos (Crete) or Benitses (Corfu), where they stay in tavernas or humbler one-star establishments. Some larger hotel complexes are dedicated to members of 18-30 Travel Clubs: sun, sea, sand, surf, sex — and alcohol.

There are numerous discos, night-clubs, floor-shows, and street-bars on holiday, as well as songboats, visits to local distilleries, so-called fish picnics, and drink-as-much-as-you-like entertainments. The temptation, or encouragement, is to drink, drink, drink, however rough the local wine, and to sleep in till noon the next day, then to spend 4 hours sunbathing in the baking heat, then to get ready for festivities all over again whilst the night is yet young. Alcohol is cheap abroad — both relatively and absolutely, except at dances and cabarets which have "free" admission but where drink must be purchased at higher-than-normal prices once inside. Many spirits distilled locally have a very high volume percentage of alcohol.

When young tourists turn up bleary-eyed at a foreign airport for the flight home, the myth is that a normal, restrained, British drinking career will be resumed immediately after the aeroplane has again supplied duty-free wines and spirits.

In fact, the holiday abroad, or occasionally on the south coast of England, has set the young single holidaymaker an increased tolerance level, **and** an increased dependency level, for alcohol. This new thirst must be sated between work-shifts and domestic chores. Frequently, the home drinking career is now busier with many new excuses to celebrate, with "just one more" and "one for the road". The seeds of addiction to alcohol, and addiction to **talking about** alcohol, have been sown.

The couriers of many holiday firms might soon be urged to reduce their plugs for alcohol, and also to refuse inducements to get their parties buying more alcohol. The pilots and cabin staff of some return flights are already almost at the point of refusing homeward passage for some half-clad teenagers; and foreign police forces are locking many British youths away overnight. Sadly, some young people have not been **in** trouble so much as **near** trouble, near to stabbings and shootings, near to riots and rampages, near to thefts and the trafficking of drugs. Their confused statements under the influence of drink are not believed.

Sixth Place: The Public House

It is appropriate to leave the public house till last because it has an ultimate attractiveness for young adults, an identity deeply rooted in history. The public house is a magnet for young drinkers — male and female — and it is constantly adapting to accommodate this affluent clientele. British public houses are spending one million pounds **a day** on renovation alone. That said, the public house cannot attract many girls under 15, or boys under 17, because of some residual lip-service to the licensing laws, and a list of prices deliberately out of the reach of many adolescents.

In 1988, the Government relaxed the licensing law of England and Wales, but only in relation to opening hours Monday to Saturday, now "liberalised" to allow any publican to open throughout the period 11am to 11pm, with Sunday lunch opening ending at 3pm. Scotland's inns were freed to open longer some years beforehand. Contrary to widespread belief, and some misinformation in Parliament, more flexible opening in Scotland **did** lead to a large increase in arrests for drunkenness and an increase of at least 15% in the alcohol consumed on licensed premises.

The restrictions affecting young people in public houses have remained largely intact since Lady Astor's bill of 1923, but all measures, new and old, were consolidated into the Licensing Act of 1964. That Act stated that "young people under 18 should not **serve** liquor to the public except in restaurants or bars serving mainly food. There is no restriction on young people aged 15 to 18 serving alcohol in supermarkets and off-licences. Part-time Saturday employment attracts many boys and girls to supermarket check-out points where they might reasonably hesitate to ask buyers **older than themselves** to put alcohol back on the shelf!.

The Act also stated that no child under 14 was to be admitted to the drinking bars of public houses during licensed hours, except specifically to eat a meal or to play in a room where no alcoholic beverages are on sale. The only significant exception to this clause was one exempting those children actually growing up in a public house.

The main clause of the 1964 Act reads: "A person under 18 may not buy, or attempt to buy, intoxicating liquor in a bar, nor may any person buy, or attempt to buy, such liquor for consumption in a bar **by** a person under 18". About the only exception is a clause allowing an unaccompanied "infant" of 16 or 17 years old to buy beer, porter, perry or cider for consumption with a meal ordered by himself or herself.

Further, it is laid down that it is a criminal offence: "knowingly to sell intoxicating liquor in a bar or out-sales department" to someone under 18. Thus under-aged drinking is one of the rare offences in English law where both the giver and the receiver, the doer and the done-to, are culpable. The 1964 Act makes the position of 16 to 17 year olds drinking in bars, and those fearful of selling to 16 and 17 year olds, unsafe. Many adolescents reject public house drinking altogether.

Price is that other deterrent. A public house has to cover its overheads — staffing, cleaning, rent, rates, interest on debt, heat, light, equipment, and the hire of equipment, as well as the costs of refurbishment and obtaining a licence — so bar prices reflect many hidden extras. Additionally, in some parts of the country, most houses are tied to a brewery, and the brewery seeks extra profits from an arrangement by which licensees agree to sell only their products in return for the tenancy. Even "Free Houses" tend to set their bar prices at what the market will stand. The average mark-up is supposed to be 30%, but in fact often exceeds 50%, making supermarket liquor very much cheaper. A few supermarkets run a brand as loss-leader just to get customers into the store to buy other drinks too.

At a point in the mid 1970s, British public houses generally conformed to one of 5 types:

1) The Coaching Inn

This would be the central residential hotel, maybe the only hotel, in a town like Stamford, Towcester or Wetherby where coaches-and-horses used to stop before rail travel became widespread.

The coaching inn has two or three bars with low ceilings, and many outhouses for the stabling of horses. It comes alive on market day in the market town of which it is the feature, the place for farmers to meet and do business. Local justices have often always permitted all-day opening for the market. Nowadays, the coaching inn may be indistinguishable from a first-class restaurant.

2) The Traditional Village Inn

Often the focal-point of the small rural village, the best known and best-loved building apart from, or next to, the Church. The place to meet and to talk, to arrange village events, and to recover from harvesting. One such village inn, The Horse and Harrow (tenants: Joe Trentfield and family), was lovingly described by John Moore in *The Brensham Trilogy* (now an Oxford Paperback), and there are many other tributes to the standard of warmth and comfort available in the village hostelry, an ideal setting for many a novel.

3) The Inner-urban Public House

This type of pub, often thrown up in the nineteenth century might be known as a "spit-and-sawdust" establishment. Its facilities are very basic: hard horse-hair seating, bare stone-flagged floors, frosted windows, vaults, and a stench of beer rising from the drains. Usually a bastion — or retreat — for males only, male manual workers — so it is sited near a large factory, a dock or a pit.

4) The New Housing Estate Public House

This is an almost deliberately featureless establishment built by brewers on the edge — or in the middle of — a vast council housing estate (itself often isolated from the town or city-centre). The housing estate public house unashamedly sells alcohol to a captive population cut off from its roots, and cut off from other areas by the paucity of public transport.

If built in the 1930s, a great decade for council-housing, this public house will be instantly recognisable by its rounded steel-framed windows, its double frontage and by its extremely functional layout. As late as the 1960s, new estate public houses would mirror the surrounding architecture to the extent of occupying a "flat" amongst flats — rather than presenting a pleasing contrast.

5) The Upgraded Urban Public House

Found in larger villages and on the outskirts of towns as well as in some city centres. Such public houses — built between 1830 and 1940 — have a Lounge and carpeted areas, and extend an invitation to women as well as men. There is softer seating and lighting, and a jollier atmosphere. Upgrading may have accompanied urban depopulation or the younger ownership of some inner-urban houses.

By the late 1960s, some breweries were attempting to renew their image by renovating and redecorating many of their tied houses, laying more carpets, building more family rooms, by hanging brasses, mounting china-shelves, and by selling bar snacks which for the first time could be counted as main meals. In 20 years, three-quarters of tied houses have become almost unrecognisable. Some have erected hand-painted signs outside, put up fairy-lights, whitewashed their walls, and provided umbrellas and wooden seats on their forecourts. There is now more chance of seeing a brass counter, a set of varied prints on the walls, a real-log-gas-fire, and an exhibition of memorabilia. Even some workers' inner-urban "hotels" have roofed their urinals and have removed their spittoons. Conversely, formerly modified public houses have uncovered and underlined real period detail.

The greatest work available on the anatomy of public houses is called: *"The Pub and The People",* now reissued as a Cresset Paperback. This massive tome is an earlier pre-War sociological investigation by Mass Observation, a group which also looked at cinemas, shops, and sports-grounds.

It is impossible here to do justice to the painstaking work of Mass Observation, in dozens of Bolton public houses, where participants sat for hours and days recording in minute detail everything from when the pieman entered the bar to when the bookie's runner visited; from the gap between ordering drinks to the gap between smoking cigarettes; from the words used by strangers to the conversation pursued by regulars; from the ambitions of volunteer bar-staff to the hopes of an annual outing to another public house! No aspect of 1930s public house life is neglected in *"The Pub and The People".* Participants were truly incognito as they sat and as they wrote. It was essential that the observers were not rumbled, and, on the fringes of illegal practices, observers ran some risks. Bolton was not so lucky keeping its anonymity. The book is well worth a read. It is a classic.

Even in the 1930s, publicans had very mixed views about young people frequenting their bars, and "young" was often taken to be 19-22 as well as 15-18. No publican wanted to lose his licence by serving anyone too young, or too likely to be a troublemaker. In fact, publicans have always retained the right to exclude anyone they choose, provided they do not contravene the Race Relations' Acts. Common signs outside inns and public houses are: "No

Hikers", "No Minibuses", "No Football Coaches", "No Singles" (curious one that), "No Motorcyclists", "No Muddy Boots", "No Travellers", "No Hawkers", "No Market Traders", "No Trainers"(!), "No Jeans", and "Couples Only". All rather arbitrary, especially the famous injunction: "Must Wear a Tie".

Public houses that assiduously **seek** teenage custom cunningly advertise themselves as open to young adults. Sometimes they have a disco-room, a Bar-B-Q., a Country and Western group or a Folk Night. Token bars in such establishments sell soft drinks only. The idea is to attract young people at the earliest opportunity. They are tomorrow's regulars. If an inn gets a name as The Place to Be, all the better. Country yokels might only drink half a pint in half a night compared with young men under 25 drinking five pints on **every visit**. Two thirds of men aged 20 to 24 visit a public house at least once a week, often with their girlfriends. Three-quarters of Oxford University under-graduates describe a Friday or Saturday evening studying at the bar as their favourite outing.

Many theme-pubs and wine bars target **women** drinkers, and young women in particular — women who might be dissatisfied with the inherent sexism of drinking in public that is dealt with below. Women drinkers are at last shedding their lace-curtain and fur-coat-smelling-of-mothballs image. New women drinkers are smart, fashionable, professional, or else **assistants** to professionals like estate agents and solicitors. They have independent incomes and no children yet. They are quite content to drink without their menfolk both at lunchtime and after work at 5.30. Nearly half of heavy-drinking women, those who drink seven units or more at one sitting, are under the age of 25 and unmarried. It is estimated that one in seven young women are physically or psychologically dependent on alcohol. So the market is huge.

One way of attracting young women is to take down the nameboard: The Nag's Head, The Red Cow or the Marquis of Granby, and replace it with a scripted: "Bijou", "The Hobbit", or "Brambles". Women are also supposed to appreciate proper powder rooms with tissue boxes on the walls, pastel shades, metal tables, wicker chairs, water colours, salad bars, no-smoking areas, and mirrors. Music must be light, cheerful, canned and unintrusive. Radio or television are out, except during Wimbledon fortnight.

Women may not always be welcome **in groups** however. This is what one West Wales publican said: "I welcome the kids coming back from college, lively and well-behaved, girls and boys alike. But the local girls with nothing to do and nowhere to go would roam our town in gangs, drinking Martini from bottles in the street before coming into the bar. Then they would shout and roar rugby songs in a pathetic imitation of the lads..."

Chauvinism and sexism run deeply in public bars, manifest especially when:

- men greatly outnumber women
- there are pornographic cuttings and calendars on display behind the bar
- women who order drinks for themselves are ignored
- women are asked to leave the public saloon in favour of the lounge
- males only serve and clear tables
- women serve behind the bar, but are stereotypical loose women ultra-glamorous, or only half-dressed for the men
- prostitutes come in and out looking for customers
- there is a "women's evening"
- vulgar and sexist jokes are told
- unattached women are leered at and chatted up
- indecent suggestions are exchanged about women's sexuality
- the entertainment is a strip-show, a kissogram, or men in drag
- the talk is all of male sport and male sporting achievements
- token women come in just to grin in admiration of their boyfriends and husbands — like stuffed dummies
- snooker, pool, skittles and darts are restricted to men only.

So women can be hounded out, especially girls in groups, because their independence and indifference to men threatens the male supremacy of the bar. Some women drinkers talk to each other not to men, and take over the dart-board or the pool table where, without men's help, they may score better. They laugh at their own jokes, not the jokes of men. They order cocktails and mixed drinks rather than huge pints of beer. They do not want to be dated. They do not want to be patronised. It is as if they are spying on the men in male territory. If some women have chosen wine-bars and women's public houses, it is because the machismo and the paternalism of male-oriented bars cannot be diminished or threatened so might as well be abandoned. Young women will not copy their grandmothers, nor sit quietly at home sewing.

Returning to the scene for **all** young people, they will get a reception in public bars dependent upon the degree of their conformity to house rules, and their ability not to upset the regulars. A headstart is given to young people from an adjacent university, young workers in full-time paid employment, the sons of regulars, steady girlfriends, and those who give the public house a good name in the locality whether for darts, pigeon-racing, charitable donations, or excellence in the Pub Quiz League. Generally, heavy drinkers will be preferred to light drinkers, provided they can "take their beer", and provided no police hunt them down, provided no glasses are stolen or fights provoked. Some publicans provide gambling machines for their young customers, or video machines where the object is to better one's performance rather than to win a jackpot. The youngster who comes in for the machines, even the cigarette machine, might well buy a lot else.

Youngsters turned away, or frowned upon, are very juvenile or rowdy, or else they sit for hours making no purchase. Alternatively, they mock and cheat bar staff, punch the publican on the nose, deface the lavatories, or they drive up on powerful motorcycles. Ironically, cyclists may be the **least** threat. Machine-riders are often bearded and in their mid 30s, but they represent an alternative and alien culture, one that will not mix with the male working ethic, the collection of heads of households evading their womenfolk. Young burglars and shoplifters "fencing" their wares might also be very unwelcome.

Each public house has its characters: those whose drinking careers are established enough to give them kudos. Round most bars will be found the Champion Drinker, the Rugby Captain, the Soapbox Philosopher, the raconteur, the joker, the spiv, the moaner, the nut-case, the womaniser, the squire, and the universal grandfather. One Athena print captures the picture superbly. A group of **cats** sit and stand round a crowded bar, each with a wonderful expression, each cat playing out a set rôle, all looking towards one or two cats for the next profundities: pub stalwarts indeed.

In Chapter Four there will be a far fuller discussion of **why** teenagers drink alcohol and why so many teenagers still choose the public house as their ideal venue. Meanwhile it is necessary to refer to Nick Dorn's key article in *Youth in Society*, January 1981: "Your Good Health".

This article was part of a bigger Alcohol in Teenage Culture

Project, and was a systematic attempt to discover how modern teenagers order their drinks, and their drinking, in public houses. Dorn advances the theory that **The Round** is central. The Round is the traditional means of purchasing liquor, and certainly not a means used only by young drinkers. One person buys a drink for everyone else in his group. The next person does the same, and so on, until everybody has bought alcohol for everybody else, whereupon everybody gets up and goes, or else a new Round is commenced.

The Round reveals **generosity;** it cuts down on **queueing;** it makes catching the barmaid's eye easier; it allows **sharing;** it displays a group's **equality;** and it soothes all customers in The Round by assuring them that they only need to **pay once** for perhaps a whole evening of drinking. In days not so long past when male dominance in drinking houses was almost complete, The Round also underlined how improper it was for women to purchase drinks whether for themselves or for others. The Round allowed for women as guests only, not hosts.

Dorn writes that many aspiring working-class youngsters no longer work in pits or large factories or quarries. Instead they work in shops, warehouses, offices and in Local Government. Aspirants may only be one or two steps up an employment ladder but they consider themselves much more fortunate than their schoolmates now working in menial occupations like gardening, cleaning and light engineering. These superior young earners behave, and drink, sociably in a manner that is not like the manner of their more manual fathers and uncles, or like the palliness of bloated executives.

When Dorn observed groups of young earners drinking in traditional surroundings, unsurprisingly he found that they embraced the virtues and values of Capitalism. That included proud use of their newly-acquired wage. They stood for independence, fairness, justice, marriage, the family, responsibility, conformity — and the importance of achievement. In pre-Thatcher days, these were the young voters to whom Thatcherism had most appeal: good common sense; pull yourself together; pull yourself up by your bootstraps; and pull your weight.

In Dorn's cliques, non-workers were not very welcome. Sometimes they were tolerated as "honorary workers", but only when they had saved up enough pocket money to stand their Round. It might take them a fortnight to do that, so once a fortnight non-workers could join their more-regular drinking acquaintances and proudly go up to the bar. Girls would either be independent earners and buy — or have bought — The Round they could pay for, or else girls would be given drinks by the boys. Dorn found that girls with very low self-esteem, with few ambitions, who had been brought up in strict and unimaginative working households, would almost always **expect** all their drinks to be bought for them.

The collectivity of the young drinking group is closely guarded. Entry is by age, spending power, daring, or by sporting achievement or attractiveness. Relatives have a head start above strangers. Spending, even by rich youngsters, must not be one-sided because that would destroy the reciprocity on which The Round depends. Gifts and favours must be exchanged, not given outright.

Dorn observed that sometimes The Round still broke down either because of the poverty of one or more members of the clique, or because of the time of week. Reciprocity could then only be **restored** by having a whip-round to buy all drinks from a central kitty, by topping up drinks rather than replacing them, or by leaving the bar prematurely. Snide comments were directed at kids, beggars, spongers or no-hopers, but low wage-earners could be excused if they still put in a full 40 hours at work.

All the young people observed craved adult status and wished to buy their alcoholic beverages the way real adults do. These young drinkers might not **really** have been privileged, but they saw themselves as relatively more successful than other youngsters, if only because they could drink in bars more openly and more regularly, and merge with their surrounds. Dorn concluded that the **How?** was more important than the **Why?** He would not separate the **cultural implications** of teenage drinking from the act of drinking. He thought that any study of norms values and attitudes had to make reference to young people's economic status without falling into the other trap of saying that young people's **main** consideration when drinking is cost and availability. He certainly saw that the public house was collective both in its smaller and larger groupings.

Summary

In this chapter, young people have been seen drinking in a variety of places where, for whatever reason, they feel it is safe to drink alcohol at an early point in their drinking careers.

Many teenagers will have had their first taste of alcohol at home, sipping from a half-empty bottle in the sideboard, opening a can when nobody else was in the house, drinking openly at a weekend family meal or joining in a celebration with assorted relatives.

Comparatively few teenagers and young adults drink alone because sociability is the overall context of drinking. This communality is evident at the street corner, on a picnic, in a party or on holiday. But each **place** of drinking yields up its own drinking behaviour. Cemetery drinking is more clandestine, even satanic, than drinking at a friend's 18th birthday. In turn, that party is much more open in the eyes of grown-ups than a West Indian drinking den or an Acid House party at a secret address. Holiday drinking is open and unrestrained, perhaps because parents are far away, but holiday drinking is anything but frivolous.

The public house keeps its position as the most desired venue for teenage drinking, although the licensing laws and high pricing make the public house more open to those over 18 than those aged 17 and under. Part of the pleasure of public house drinking is that it may be forbidden officially. Another pleasure is sociability at the most sociable period of young people's lives.

The public house also acts as an agent for **socialisation**: triple socialisation — preparing to enter **adult** society, preparing to enter adult **male** society, and preparing to enter adult **drinking** society. The public house is the college for those embarking upon their drinking careers. It is full of mysteries and rituals, ways and means, shady dealings and open dealings.

The most popular and longstanding rite is The Round which can be compared in schooling with reading round the class, standing up in turn, each mounting the buck, or answering specific questions in alphabetical succession. As in the classroom, or gymnasium, nobody is expected to escape The Round.

Some young people, young women in particular, can however escape the traditional partriarchal or paternalistic public house. They can vote with their feet and converge in droves at new winebars called "Fidelity", or "Last Resort". Alternatively, they can enjoy the greater comforts of theme bars: "Dickens", or "Steam Nostalgia". Young people wish to maintain their own culture even in the alien surroundings of the traditional downtown public house, and this can cause (thinly concealed) inter-generational hostility.

Sometimes, young drinkers have nothing new to say or do and so slip quietly into the drinking habits and social expectations of their elders.

CHAPTER FOUR

Discovering the Motive

Use, John, use, John, winks at this abuse, John,
And when you recommend the pledge,
Will patch up some excuse, John:
Many drink because they're cold, and some because they're hot
  John;
Many drink because they're cold, and some because they're not
  John;
Many drink because they're thin, and some because they're stout,
  John;
Many drink because they're in, and some because they're out, John!
"Nay!" John, "Nay!" John,
That's what you must say, John.
Whenever you are asked to drink,
Or you'll be led astray, John!

from the Temperance Melodist, 1891

All the drinking needed to keep the human body alive can safely be contained within ten minutes each day: ten drinks gulped down in 60 seconds or five drinks each imbibed in 120 seconds. So what makes young people, especially, attach so much importance to drinking alcohol — and spend so long drinking alcohol — is something of a puzzle. If the answer is not simple **thirst,** what is it? Nobody can ever be sure of the true impulse, the propulsion, the compulsion, to drink — because teenagers are no more likely to tell their elders why they are doing what they are doing than they are to have a ready explanation for their joy-riding, their lengthy phone-calls to friends they saw half an hour ago, their truancy, their cat-burgling, their hobbies, their reading or their sexual proclivities.

That leaves adults, parents, teachers, social workers and publicans **guessing** at what makes young people drink alcohol, and drink it in such quantities, whilst accepting without hesitation that teenage drinking is no aberration, certainly not an **abnormal** thing to be doing.

The almost complete acquiescence of grown-ups to their children's intoxication is paradoxical at first sight, because normally there is **moral panic** surrounding young people who hit each other with chains, who knock down little old ladies, who slash themselves with razor blades, who congregate in large numbers at seaside resorts, who drop litter, who swear, who shout down speakers on a public platform, or who take "hard" drugs.

The benign sideways glance of policemen, magistrates, parents and figures of authority towards teenage drinking is not lost on the teenagers themselves. They soon grasp that adults in general, and responsible adults in particular, are extremely ambivalent. Most adults are moderate drinkers in their own right and are reticent to intervene, as will be seen in Chapter Six. Even less prepared are they to debar their children's consumption of alcohol.

A similar double bind, a similar double-standard, affecting the Government's attitude towards young drinkers will also be explored in the Conclusion. There has not been a Royal Commission on Alcohol for many decades. Royal Commissions generally are out of favour. The nearest thorough exploration of drinking behaviour in Britain was a report from the Government's "Think Tank" — otherwise known as the Central Policy Review Staff (now disbanded) — in the late 1970s. The completed report was so sensitive, so radical in its conclusions, so hard-hitting in its criticism of Government attitudes to alcohol, that it was suppressed by both Labour and Conservative administrations. Commentators kept on expecting a report to appear, but the Think Tank's deliberations would have been secret for ever had not a smuggled report eventually seen the light of day in Sweden!

In November 1987, however, the Home Office Standing Conference on Crime Prevention issued its report on "Young People and Alcohol". Also the Government made a half-hearted attempt to resurrect an inter-departmental discussion on alcohol in the form of the "Howe/Wakeham Committee on Alcohol Abuse" — named after 2 successive Leaders of the House of Commons: John Wakeham and Sir Geoffrey Howe.

Obviously, as with the **amount** of drinking, survey staff always rely heavily on self-report, but self-report on **reasons** for drinking yields an 80% reply — "for enjoyment", which may not get interviewers a lot further. "For enjoyment", however, though a bland and uninformative reply, does link teenage drinking firmly with the enjoyment teenagers always seek everywhere. Therefore, enjoyment enters into all other reasons listed below.

Motive One: Adulthood

The search for adulthood was suggested in young people's occupancy of the benches of public houses. This motive covers:

- observing drinking adults
- envying drinking adults
- accompanying drinking adults
- viewing drinking adults on television
- tolerating drunken parents and older siblings
- sharing jokes about other drinking adults
- buying alcohol for drinking adults
- imitating drinking adults
- excusing drinking adults
- changing home routines or personal leisure time to accommodate drinking adults
- offering to serve adults with another drink.

Young people imbibe the culture of adult drinking from a very early age, as if they were actually being brought up in a public house (the fate of several thousand children). By age 3 or 4, most toddlers understand that drink is not all harmless. Some drink comes in funny containers and decanters. Some drinks are poured into peculiar-shaped glasses over lumps of ice. Some drinks are to be feared. Some are to be kept on the very top shelf of the larder. Some drinks appear only when relations call. Some drinks are not to be touched, never mind tasted.

As with smoking, children discover: that is what adults do when they are grown-up enough, just like sleeping in double beds, playing cards late at night, taking the driving test, or shooting pheasants. The child who "jumps the gun" and starts shooting the cat at age six is excused his premature adulthood (which is nonetheless worrying).

Motive Two: Maturation

Maturation is linked to the childhood search for adulthood, but is by now much closer to the fulfilment of that dream:

- being allowed one's first Babycham
- having courage to sip Mum's sherry when her back is turned
- illicitly sharing a can of lager behind the bike-shed
- going to one's first grown-up party
- being served in a public bar with no questions asked
- attaining the age of 18
- getting tipsy or drunk for the very first time
- being included (as an apprentice) in one's first office party
- having one's first alcohol bought by a new boyfriend
- buying a first ever round with lots of 10 penny pieces
- drinking a glass of wine with parents in a restaurant.

It matters not whether maturation has actually been reached, so long as it *appears* to have been reached. A discerning adult can distinguish between the heavy make-up, lipstick, powder and mascara that has made an older woman seem younger, and that which has made quite a young teenage girl seem much older. Maturation is all about wearing masks, gaining new identities: the first braces, the first pair of designer-jeans, the first shave, the first high-heels, the first freedom to come in alone at midnight on a Saturday night. Within such a process of maturation, the 18th Birthday might actually be a disappointment.

Motive Three: Employment

This motive lies behind much of the drinking undertaken by young people aged between 18 and 25:

- drinking as a mark of new earning capacity
- drinking at the end of a shift
- drinking **during** the night-shift
- drinking at the lunch break
- drinking to meet new business acquaintances
- drinking to strengthen relations with colleagues
- drinking to find out information (perhaps for journalism)
- drinking to keep up with former schoolfriends now also employed locally
- drinking in the position of servant, nanny or babysitter in another person's house

- accepting a drink during home visits (eg. social work)
- drinking because "everyone else" does at work
- drinking at the buffet before interviews
- drinking for a dare during a Youth Training Scheme
- drinking during postings as a member of the Armed Services
- drinking during stints behind the bar.

It needs to be noted here that a large number of employers share society's perplexity as to how to approach teenage drinking. A complete ban on alcohol in the factory or office is relatively easy to enforce, but what about midday drinking in the public house next to the firm's headquarters? What about the managers' canteen? What happens when the company has just won an important new order and everybody wants to toast to future prosperity? The drunken young employee is not difficult to recognise, but what about a new recruit who has just had a beaker-full?

Motive Four: Taste

Taste is a word applied more perhaps to food and to gastronomic treats than to drink and rare punches, but in the latter context, taste shows in:

- actually enjoying alcoholic beverages
- needing a glass of whisky or sherry at a certain time each day
- needing a glass of wine to bring out the flavour of food
- experimenting with various cocktails and concoctions
- finding that alcohol "does the body good"
- finding certain spirits warming
- craving the sensation of a drink actually passing down the throat
- claiming some finesse or expertise in wine-tasting
- always having the beer to accompany the sandwiches
- turning to alcohol first to quench thirst
- savouring alcohol as an aperatif.

That said, several teenagers report back that they do not actually **like** the taste of lager, or their first glass of sherry. They say they feel empty or all fizzed up, gurgling, constipated — or even sick. Alcohol in quantity cannot rest happily with food, or absence of food, because of the frequency of vomiting after drinking. Expectations can be far more satisfying than the fulfilment of the same. Under pressure, teenagers might accept a shandy or a cider, but privately they say they would have preferred a bitter lemon or pure apple juice. Taste is something very personal.

Motive Five: Peer-Group Pressure

Undoubtedly the pressure of mates, contemporaries and drinking partners influences many youthful drinkers:

- going to the public house when everybody else does
- vying to be served in a bar, younger than anyone else
- going to a drinks' party with the crowd
- buying alcohol on the recommendation of a friend
- buying — or drinking alcohol — to impress friends
- drinking to win, or to keep, the affections of one particular boyfriend or girlfriend
- helping to consume a six-pack on the riverbank
- drinking in playtime, between lessons
- drinking to enhance observed masculinity
- drinking with colleagues at work, or to unwind after work
- social drinking by invitation
- not wanting to turn down an invitation
- not wanting to be left out of the crowd, or left behind
- drinking on a coach-outing
- or when placed in the position of no soft drinks being on offer, or even for sale.

Peer-group pressure has to be handled delicately because that same pressure can sustain **abstinence** as well as intoxication. The Temperance Movement harnessed friendship and companionship to enlist youngsters first to sign the pledge, then to remain teetotal. Equally, a band of modern sixth-formers or youth club attenders may organise their week to cut out alcohol, not to leave any room for it. The same might apply to a dry girl's hockey team, or an evangelical church with no permit to have alcohol available. One non-drinking clique might share the same set of abstaining parents.

Also, the notion of peer-group pressure can be demeaning to certain young people, as if they do not possess minds of their own, as if they are governed by herd instinct, roaming with the pack. It is all rather determinist or fatalistic. Groups do indeed matter more to teenagers than to 40-year-olds or retired persons, but many teenagers retain a keen sense of individuality. Even within a football stadium, each young supporter can be backing his team in a different way. One girl will be cheering; another jeering the opposing team. One boy will be blowing up his inflatable banana; another rattling his rattle. One girl will throw an unravelled toilet roll in sheer joy at a goal scored; another will stretch her bright acrylic scarf above her head. One boy will memorise the programme; another will be arguing that his team do not deserve to win on today's performance. They are not a **uniform** crowd. Superficially the young supporters **look** alike because they are similarly dressed and standing near each other. Just as all supporters do not taunt the police or pinch unsuspecting garden gnomes on the way home from a match, so all young drinkers do not fight, or fight for more liquid refreshment.

Motive Six: Sexuality

Already in Chapter Two, the sexual appeal of drinking was mentioned:

● drinking with a partner before sleeping with her
● drinking with an acquaintance before **hoping** to sleep with her
● drinking to attract the attention of one special boy or girl
● going to a public bar and ordering a pint of beer as definite proof of masculinity
● drinking in a Gay Bar or a Gay Club
● drinking in a group before the group is split into separate couples
● party drinking between spells of light or heavy petting
● party drinking to give **courage** for sexual advances
● sexual carelessness following drinks
● drinking whilst telling — or listening to — jokes with an explicit sexual content
● drinking whilst listening to sexually suggestive music
● drinking as a consolation for sexual failure, rejection, or unattractiveness.

When the **sexism** inherent in public drinking is so often ignored, one might expect the **sexuality** of young drinking to be readily understood. In fact, many sexual messages transmitted during the consumption of alcohol are not picked up or decoded. Those messages do not reach the consciousness even of the **sender.**

Sufficient to remember that sexuality, even sexual aversion, reticence and revulsion, is common to all adolescents. Sexuality fills many daytime dreams and night-time fantasies. Sexuality is youth's driving force and does not diminish after the age of 21.

Indeed, as young people defer marriage until the late 20s, many more young people are unattached, or cohabiting, for several years in which case they can continue drinking at the same level as their 16 and 17 year old brothers and sisters. Drink can literally be a come-on.

Motive Seven: Escape from Boredom

Unlike the motives mentioned so far, this is a negative intention, actually to get a way from a condition of mind:

- attending a party for excitement
- drinking at a Pop-festival for excitement
- drinking secretly or with one close friend for thrills
- going to a public house because there is "nowhere else to go"
- being bored in a public bar rather than being bored at home
- hoping that public house conversation will be less boring than the usual adult conversation
- being fed up sitting indoors in front of the television
- tired of looking after a very young baby
- drinking during unemployment
- drinking in the park or on the street corner as a way to fill time
- pub-crawling as a way to meet different beers and different cronies
- drinking after a day revising for examinations
- drinking to survive a dead-end job at some conveyor belt
- drinking in a foyer, lounge or public house whilst waiting for an acquaintance to arrive or to keep an appointment. This is something for idle hands to do. Hands are not much use unless they are holding something or reaching out for something. Glass-in-hand **looks** right and guarantees some privacy into the bargain.

Again, the concept of boredom must be handled with caution. On the exterior, it would appear absurd that the generation with most pop records, most personal stereos, must fun fairs, most magazines, most television receivers, most photocopiers in the classroom, most paperbacks, most private transport and most job-creation schemes, could ever be bored. There are so many stimuli. But bored many young people are, bored not just today but also yesterday and tomorrow, bored not just at school, but also on holiday. Boredom in fact has become a habit and an expectation. There is no life after boredom. Boredom condemns the teenager to bed all Saturday morning.

Motive Eight: Making the Body Feel Better
Teenagers share this motive with adult drinkers:

- drinking to dispel depression
- drinking to relieve a hangover!
- drinking to reduce stress
- drinking as part of mental disorientation
- drinking in response to "the sick-building syndrome"
- drinking for uplift
- drinking for sedation after a tragedy or a disappointment
- drinking after being diagnosed terminally ill
- drinking to absorb pain
- drinking alcohol to feed the body's dependency
- drinking to supplement — or to counteract — other drugs
- drinking instead of taking tranquillizers.

As observed in the next chapter, the use of alcoholic beverages to improve personal health is an elusive goal. Temporary elation is followed by drowsiness. High spirits are followed by low spirits. Digestion becomes indigestion. A desire for just one more drink intensifies the nausea it was intended to alleviate. New headaches rack the brain.

The body eventually rejects the alcohol by spewing it up or combining it with urine and sweat. Or else the body tolerates alcohol and seeks even more. The alcohol meant to cure one illness causes another. So health might become a spiral downwards. Sometimes people refer to "a complete breakdown of health". Poor health degenerates into poorer health.

Alcohol is a curious substance because it **does** have authentic (though often overstated) medicinal properties. It helps those whose joints have stiffened and whose recovery from a serious operation is delayed. Brandy can calm someone in a state of clinical shock. The debate as to whether alcohol is a "drug" or not will go on. The word "drug" is perhaps too medical, and is certainly confusing, whereas the term "harmful substance", is more widely applicable, and fits more neatly into the determination of some heavy drinkers as "problem drinkers" rather than "alcoholics".

Motive Nine: Availability

Mallory once explained that he was about to climb Everest "because it's there". So some young people:

- drink the alcohol laid on at weddings
- drink the alcohol freely ladled out at parties
- drink at a gathering where every participant has brought a bottle
- drink what they can discover in the parental cocktail cabinet
- drink the alcoholic beverages they see advertised
- drink on holiday as part of the excursion-price
- drink on expense account
- drink when treated by customers in a bar
- drink where there is a public house next door
- drink when their parents are in the licensed trade
- drink where supermarkets have special offers
- drink when eating at a friend's house
- drink on aeroplanes and ferries where prices are cut
- drink to finish up a bottle.

We shall never know whether availability can be an influence or a motive by itself. Many would argue that availability is an incidental factor, that the non-drinker could not possibly become a drinker "just because it's there". Further, they would suggest that drinkers are already **predisposed** to the alcohol. That they do not turn their backs on availability is a sign of personal weakness.

There is, however, a certain **inertia** about drinking. So many avenues are opened socially by alcohol, and so universal is its availability at important functions that availability **alone** might become a temptation too strong to resist, almost like an impulse purchase when shopping. Very few shoppers have a shopping-list so precise that it allows no supplementation or deviation. Many parties have always been alcoholic. Many election campaigns have always been fought in local hostelries. Many students' unions have always focussed on the buttery. Many supermarkets have the widest aisles and the most laden shelves in their drinks' departments.

When in Rome it really does pay to do as Rome does: not to break the norms of polite company. With conformity comes stability. Availability is not accidental. It is there as an enticement, and as an inducement. Young people, like their elders, believe there **is** such a thing as a free lunch, so they cannot believe their luck when they arrive somewhere where drink is on tap and unlikely to run out.

Travelling along tram-lines is much easier than tracking across dunes. The drinking of brightly-packaged and heavily promoted alcoholic beverages is a marketing director's dream — even when the drinker has not had to pay for his drink.

Motive Ten: To Get Drunk

This explicit motive — complete intoxication — is different from the escape from boredom. Some teenagers want to:

- show off being drunk
- prove their capacity for alcohol
- drink in competition with the best of them
- win a drinking contest
- drink themselves under the table
- drink heavily against the clock
- complete the celebration of a birthday, the birth of a new baby, by not leaving **until** drunk
- drink away a windfall
- drown sorrow conclusively
- gain pity after being jilted
- acquire an excuse for rowdiness, and the settling of old scores
- forget recently served bad examination results or decrees for divorce
- round off a national festival or royal occasion
- anticipate a wedding
- celebrate a wedding ostentatiously
- get drunk to do justice to Christmas-time
- get drunk because it is Saturday night
- get drunk as there is no point returning to an empty home
- get drunk as a **culmination** of an evening's drinking
- get drunk as compensation for being given notice at work
- get drunk because of a great victory for the team
- get drunk in order to be cossetted and carried home.

Drunkenness is a very specific phenomenon, also a very medical condition, even a fatal condition where intoxication exceeds the upper limit of safety, where intoxication accompanies drug addiction, or where the drunkard chokes, or falls in freezing cold weather, with no assistance at hand.

At the same time, drunkenness is not the same as alcohol-dependence, although the two go hand-in-hand in certain individuals. Only an overdose of a prescribed drug, or experimentation with prohibited drugs, can produce a sensation quite like drunkenness — putting oneself beside oneself, revelling in total disorientation. Drunkenness is to be transported away, to carry the mind out of the body which imprisons it, to explore new territory, to release one's true character, to loosen the tongue, in fact to assume a new identity, less nervous, less shy, less careworn, less a failure, less ugly, less inconsistent, less impatient. So drunkenness answers both the heights of success and the depths of failure. Drunkenness cements and fractures the best of relationships.

In her very moving book: *Beyond Fear* (Fontana 1987), psychologist Dorothy Rowe goes into great detail about young people's **suppressed** fears and anxieties, the postponed, therefore unresolved, emotional tensions of their early childhoods. She asserts that many young people have **not** been wanted or well looked after. Their parents have not put the children's needs before the needs of the adults in the home. Nor have parents **listened** intently to their children. Many children have thus grown up damaged, blaming themselves for having been naughty, blaming themselves for having been beaten, molested and neglected. It follows, in Dorothy Rowe's reasoning, that as soon as young people attain some measure of adolescent autonomy, they drink — and get drunk — to quell the lingering uncertainties of years gone by. Often children have never related their inmost fears to **anyone.**

Drunkenness is one of the only **legal** escape mechanisms available to young people, a tenth of whom are drinking to escape various pressures in any case. It is more often the subject of ribaldry than of condemnation, more often the subject of inclusiveness than ostracism, more often the ingredient of unfolding drama than the calamity that spoils the drama. Society has to condone drunkenness, at least the drunkenness of its young meteors, stockbrokers, pop-stars, accolites and Hooray-Henrys, because society condones alcohol in its less exhibitionist drapery. Besides, young people are exhibitionists in any case. For them to be drunk is to occupy the centre of the stage for a few minutes, to follow a new script, to adopt new rôles, acting, and reacting, uncharacteristically, unpredictably and unrestrainedly.

The attractiveness of drunkenness for teenagers begins with **the language** of intoxication. Here are just a few of the more polite synonyms for drunkenness in the colourful language of alcohol:

tight/plastered/paralytic/sozzled/sloshed/stoned
inebriated/bowled over/out for the count/

Brahms and Liszt/fiddled/up to the eyeballs/
muzzled/elevated/groggy/bosky/top-heavy/squiffy/
merry/primed/oiled/parallel/canned/flushed/tanked (up)

There is even a fine distinction between being drunk and being "blind drunk". In one large youth club sample, 28% of respondents said they get drunk occasionally, 21% frequently.

Very young children fear madness and drunkenness as common evils. Older children differentiate between the two, but may still dread drunkenness because for them it means a hiding, a pasting, a terrible row, overhearing a terrible row, being dragged out of bed, being sent round to the neighbours, being sexually molested, having to sleep with a drunken father or stepfather, having the house smashed up, witnessing mother being beaten up, being neglected, undernourished, locked away, or sent to bed before time.

So drunkenness is not an inviting prospect **until** adolescence, and then only for a proportion of adolescents who foresee a new piece of forbidden territory, something to boast about, the ultimate mind-bender after so many recent mind-bending experiences: the white-knuckle rides at the fair, the uncontrolled descent of steep and twisting water-shoots, orgasm or ejaculation in the middle of petting, wind-surfing, riding a cycle downhill without brakes, abseiling, and watching the most numbing and excruciating horror-movies and horror videos. Yes, adolescence is about letting the self escape towards selfhood. Most mind-bending is harmless, or at worst irritating and temporarily to be regretted. Drunkenness however is the next category of absent-mindedness on. Not a few children of drunkards grow up to become drunkards and to pass on the chain of cruelty to their own sober offspring. Perhaps drunkenness is not much fun after all.

Summary

The ten motives for teenage drinking outlined in this chapter do not form a comprehensive list. Many other motives impinge upon drinking. Nor is each reason for drinking alcohol mutually **exclusive.** The measure of the motive cannot be calculated in isolation from other motives. It is possible to be bored **and** to want to make one's body function better; it is possible to act like an adult **and** quench thirst after digging the garden; it is possible to attract the opposite sex at the same time as yielding to peer-group pressures.

Celebration is a bolt holding nearly all the nuts together.

Celebrating is supposed to be a holy activity, but often becomes debased and unholy. Celebration is the occasion for a flight from boredom, for a yielding to the pressure of the group, for new sexual liaisons and for demonstrating maturation. Celebrations are as numerous as double the number of one's acquaintances, as each person has a birthday once a year, and each has at least one other high-point each year — like the birth of a niece or promotion at work, or a refund.

Drunkenness also binds all other motives together as it is the conclusion, the extreme, of all other drinking behaviour, relating to boredom, maturity, enjoyment, pain, showing off and going out with work-mates. Drunkenness is happiness and unhappiness.

Throughout this chapter I have used the words ''motives'' and ''reasons'' advisedly in preference to the terms ''causes'' and ''excuses''. Motivation is frequently unconscious, so young people can be excused for not telling the barmaid why they have just ordered another drink, and for not telling their parents why they have just come home reeking of drink, and for not elaborating on the answer: ''I drink because it's enjoyable''. Better to reserve judgment as to whether peer-group pressure is the **paramount** reason for teenage drinking. There is many a slip between cup and lip.

CHAPTER FIVE

Discovering the Alternative

You are brave, and wise, and gifted;
You can row both safe and fast;
You can steer amid temptation,
Sunken rock, or stormy blast.
Kindle too, the lighthouse beacon;
Flash its rays across the wave:
You may warn and guide the drifting —
Save the drunkard, save, oh, save!

Bravely launch the Temperance lifeboat
On the stormy sea of life;
Come, ye strong and daring, man her —
Fearless in the tempest strife.

from the Temperance Melodist, 1891.

There are several alternatives for young people wanting, or tempted, to drink alcohol. The strength or weakness of these alternatives rests on their ability to act as full substitutes for alcohol. Alternatives must not merely quench thirst. A longing for company and ambience and excitement, in fact access to the full range of emotions converging with intoxication, must be satisfied, and **positively.**

Alternative A:
Non-Alcoholic Beverages on Licensed Premises
Many young people have already caught on to this possibility. Nine out of ten adolescents are aware that soft drinks are available in public houses, and seven out of ten know that some beers and lagers

now have an infinitesimal amount of pure alcohol. Boys in a mixed group can often be seen carrying trays half full of alcoholic beverages for some of the boys, half full of non-alcoholic drinks for some of the girls — though gender differences are increasingly being eroded or reversed.

One difficulty with this alternative is **price.** Breweries often own a subsidiary bottling plant for soft drinks and it is these soft drinks that they sell to tied public houses. The brewers insist on either the same mark-up for fizzy, juices and squashes, or a **higher** mark-up to deter young revellers, or to promote more profitable lines like Martini and gin-and-tonics. Thus, in 1989 prices, a tiny bottle of pineapple juice (15 or 20ml.) can cost as much at 55p as a full litre in the supermarket (59p). Perrier water in a bar can cost 90p, in a supermarket 24p. Coca-Cola costs up to 85p for a third of a litre in the bar, as against 14 to 18p in many supermarkets. Some bars charge 20p for one squirt of orange squash, or 50p for adding lemonade to grapefruit juice. True comparisons would need to be made on **wholesale** prices, in which case the cost to the young drinker could easily be **ten** times the cost to the publican.

A second difficulty is **authenticity.** There are still teenage pressures exerted on each other to "drink something proper". Even some adults have tried to dissuade their 19 or 20 year-old sons from choosing a soft drink. Occasionally soft drinks are laced for fun, so that teenagers are tricked into drinking more alcohol than they have ordered. One-sixth of a gill of apple juice looks very similar to one-sixth of a gill of whisky, and a frothing Pepsi-Cola could be mistaken in dim lighting for half a pint of bitter. But few drinkers are deceived. Mockers soon pick up a lack of backbone in soft-drinkers (the very word soft is unhelpful). Girls might be excused, but that merely emphasises the sexism rife in public bars. It takes a very plucky teenager to swim against the tide **every** night.

A third impediment is **the drinking environment.** If teenagers, or young adults, drink soft drinks in a public house, they are still supporting the brewers, the drinking culture, the rules and norms of the public house, and the primacy of alcohol in leisure. They are even condoning the incipient problem-drinking of some of their contemporaries. One might as well go to a race meeting to sunbathe, go to a Mozart concert to sleep, or go to the seaside to have five hours in a good department store. Worse, one is at a race meeting to make a point that gambling is foolish. One is studying at university to make the point that personality counts, not academic attainment.

Alternative B:
Coffee-bars in the High Street

In the 1950s there was a possibility that National Milk Bars would become the main venue for teenagers at leisure. As a second best there would be Wimpy Houses or transport cafés. This was also the decade when motor scooters were going to become the main form of youth transport.

For a while, Italian-style Expresso coffee-bars caught on. They appeared, principally in London, then they disappeared. Young people were obviously not going to emulate their Continental pen-friends, least those young people in Switzerland who think nothing of having a coffee and gateau late at night. There looked to be no viable alternative to the public house — not even Kentucky Fried Chicken because their outlets had so little seating.

Then to the rescue came burger-bars like McDonalds, brightly-coloured shops open late selling everything in brightly-coloured cardboard cartons. Such establishments usually open under franchise, imports from the United States. Burger-bars do not pay well but their staff have great flexibility with the shifts they can best work, and burger-bars rarely turn customers away even if they have only ordered one hot chocolate and have sat for ¾ of an hour. That is to their credit. Young people do have some choice of unlicensed premises even if they pop in just before or after using licensed premises as well.

Alternative C:
Non-Alcoholic Bars

The idea here is to capture the **atmosphere** of a public house with none of the temptations, or inebriation. Quite a few youth-clubs, youth-wings, church crypts and sixth-form common rooms have been adapted to resemble drinking bars, even theme-pubs. There was even an experiment in Horsham to have a full non-alcoholic public house, but it had to shut due to threats of drunkenness!

More longlasting are the teenage bars of conventional public houses where there are discos and groups. There is considerable potential at seaside resorts and in city centres to open up these wings, especially when so many public houses have far more upper-rooms and bedrooms than they can ever use.

Sadly, vandals often give the foam-filled plastic seating of their youth-club bar the unkindest cut of all, and limited funding always makes these pretend-bars look like second-best.

Young people can sniff out condescension from miles off, whether it is the vicar turning up on a motorcycle or their own parents learning the twist, or teachers protesting that everybody in class has equal influence. Pubs-with-no-beer are especially suspect. Youngsters do not want adults underlining their immaturity, treating them as children (a stage of life now firmly behind them).

Alternative D:
Sport, Sportiness, and Sports' Centres

Superficially this is an extremely attractive alternative to alcohol intake. Many municipalities have gone ahead and opened multi-purpose leisure centres with squash-courts and table tennis tables that can be booked a week in advance, centres which have a resident under-18 swimming club, a 5-a-side league and a basketball team.

The Sports' Council slogan: SPORT FOR ALL, was not however well-received when it was discovered that **All** meant all who owned a car and consulted their filofax organisers 10 days before they required exercise, and who shelled out £180 for designer-sportswear before meeting the hire charge of £2.50 per hour.

Nevertheless, most young people have an undeniable and undying interest in sport, as spectators if not as participants. Sport **could** be a distraction from alcohol were it not for:

- sporty people playing then drinking
- sports personalities drinking heavily
- sports spectators drinking heavily
- some breweries sponsoring sporting events
- some leading sportsmen advertising alcohol
- some sports like rugby becoming synonymous with drinking
- sports clubs opening their own bars
- sports centres opening their own bars
- swimming pools having a bar in the gallery
- many golf-club-houses acting as ''The Nineteenth Hole''
- many team supporters relying on drink during travel
- many sports stadia advertising drink on perimeter fencing
- winners boasting their performance in the public house.

Thus the whole stratagem can back-fire. Sportiness has definitely not recovered its school-days motto: ''Mens Sana in Corpore Sano''.

Alternative E:
The Healthy Life-Style

This alternative became far more realisable, far more diversionary and far more attractive in the 1980s. If lifestyle is a statement about self, then healthy lifestyle is a statement about healthy self, with few of the negative connotations of "Muscular Christianity", the brand of faith endorsed by Charles Kingsley and F.D. Maurice in the last century, having the proverbial Dr. Thomas Arnold as chief exponent.

The exclamation: "I feel good!" need not come only from the lips of the teenager who has just run 26 miles along a tarmacadam road, or who is bulging with muscles from a recent course in weightlifting. The healthy lifestyle is a combination of good sleep, foods rich in vitamins and fibre, reasonable exercise, time out-of-doors, relaxation, herbal remedies, skin-care and the rejection of harmful substances.

"Holism" is the belief that the body functions best when viewed as a whole rather than as a series of symptoms and ailments, hence holistic medicine which targets the whole person. The healthy lifestyle fulfils holistic goals, mind and body working in partnership.

The healthy, whole, young person does not drink alcohol except lightly and occasionally, maybe with a special meal or at Christmas. She has something else to think about and to be proud of — being wholesome and trying to find environmentally-friendly solutions to some local and national issues. Such an aim has inbuilt satisfaction and justification. So alcohol is largely redundant.

It should be stressed though that the healthy lifestyle is not naïvely utopian or rigidly joyless. It is not the product of Deep South fundamentalism or Massachusetts' social psychology. It is a trunk road rather than an immediate destination.

Alternative F:
The Armed Forces

This alternative always has currency whenever unruly young people are in the news. Conscription is the universal solution, but less now that it has been scrapped for 30 years and never reintroduced.

As a cure for alcohol-dependence the armed forces cannot meet the bill. The discipline is there for young recruits — perhaps too much — and militarism still implies some status-degradation. But soldiers, the squaddies, and sailors on shore-leave are some of the **heaviest** drinkers and the wildest young men around town. Alcohol has always buttressed National Service and troops serving in remote outposts like the Falkland Islands report sporadic fighting among their numbers after barrack-room drinking.

Alternative G:
A Change of Friends

If friendship is indeed the key to why young people drink, then there is a possibility that they will drastically reduce alcohol consumption when they acquire an alternative set of friends: a group who do not visit public houses nightly or weekly, a group which divorces itself from the drinking culture.

Again this option is initially attractive, until it dawns that teenagers are notably indignant at having friends chosen **for** them. In fact, they bitterly resent any interference in this area of their lives. They rebel against parental matches; and parental disapproval **reinforces** their choice of "unsuitable" friend or peer-group. Any adolescent sub-group is bonded by the common enemy. Disgrace, or a fall from grace, acts like cement.

Only when the young person **herself** decides she needs a change of company, or a change of activity, will she look further afield.

Alternative H:
An Alternative Hobby

This also sounds fine in theory. After all, drinking is a hobby, for some young people an occupation that fills all their leisure time after homework and hair-wash. A new hobby like stamp-collecting, orienteering, angling, or folk-dancing could broaden the perspective, even displace alcohol.

Predictably, many young people are no more receptive to having their hobbies chosen for them than having their friendships and marriages arranged. They are especially resistant to the "good idea to fill up your time". Young people treat with suspicion the Duke of Edinburgh Award, Scouts, nature walks, even youth clubs, unless they are already **affiliated**. Detached adolescents seem to be detached from **everything**, joining nothing.

Many young people have followed their parents' hobbies since being young children, hobbies like rambling, bird-watching, and canals, in which case teenage years are when this **inherited** interest will either be discarded or translated into a personal interest in its own right. If drinking has been an absent or insignificant leisure activity for parents, it may naturally become the same for certain teenagers.

The state, and the local council — right from the days of the Roman emperors — have also had a say in young people's leisure pursuits. Leisure has not been the equivalent of **pleasure.** Society has wanted to organise, channel and divert leisure activities. This governance has also stretched to leisure **days** like Sundays and feast-days. So working people have always needed ingenuity to subvert leisure facilities and leisure suggestions to conform with "antisocial", but far more enjoyable, goals. Thus park lakes are very good for ship-wrecks; airwaves are ideal for pirate-radio; bonfires can burn effigies; and libraries are the finest stamping-group going for hide-and-seek.

Take a group, or a family of young people to the seaside and they will amuse themselves in a way incomprehensible to parents and grand-parents: diving and splashing, not swimming; penny slot-machines, not buckets and spades; dodgem rides rather than donkey rides; skateboarding, not skipping. Pastimes are just that: they pass the time. Drinking is often a **pre-eminent** pastime because it rides on the back of so many diverse hobbies that at first do not have an alcoholic dimension. Graveyards, the ultimate leisure resort, are for the living as well as the dead. Get a child studying epitaphs and......

Alternative I−:
Gettting Married and Settling Down

This alternative is often presented to "dolly birds" and to "lager louts" who have just stolen a motorcycle, terrorised a local fish-and-chip shop owner, or who have run naked down the white lines of the main road from cat's-eye to cat's-eye.

The idea is also suggested to young people who have outstayed their welcome at home, who have not picked up hints about flying from the nest, and who still demand "everything found" including 21 cooked meals a week. Perhaps the heavy-metal music blaring from four speakers has not been turned down. The poll-tax return has not been filled in, and life is a constant queue for the bathroom, a never-ending shouting match.

Of course, the proposition that any boy should "get on his bike", or settle down presupposes that:

● he has a close relationship with a member of the opposite sex
● he wants a heterosexual marriage
● he endorses belief in a male-dominated relationship where the

woman uncomplainingly gets on with the domestic chores
- he has spending power only for alcohol **or** marriage
- he is emotionally prepared for the commitment that marriage entails
- he wants only a very short gap between the wedding and the birth of the first baby.

"Settling down" is something teenagers will indeed do, but only after they have explored different relationships and countries and lifestyles, and only when they have saved up. Saving up nowadays is difficult because house prices, even furniture and carpeting prices, and rents, exceed earning potential by such a wide margin. Besides, many young adults, at least a quarter, live with a partner for some months or years before plunging into marriage. These years may be spent in a squat or in a multiple-occupancy house, and drinking will **still** be prevalent. If it is a girl marrying, she may not tolerate her man returning at the first opportunity to meet his bachelor friends at the public house. She'll go as well or ask him to stay and drink in front of the video-taperecorder. "Settling down" might actually involve quite lavish entertaining, too.

Alternative J:
Finding a Different Substance

How many parents now rue the day that they weaned a youngster off tobacco. At the time, it seemed so logical. Smoking was using up all her pocket-money, turning her fingers yellow, and making her cough and splutter. Could she not find a better use for her finances? Why not suck a humbug or keep some cheese-straws at hand?

Young people have discarded tobacco in favour of alcohol, or started to "graze" instead of chain-smoking. Trouble occurs however when the young ex-smoker **also** goes for excessive alcohol consumption. Once the new habit is confirmed, the old habit returns! So there is twice the problem. Coming off alcohol works in favour of Ecstasy (an amphetemine-like drug peddled among young people). The problem is doubled when there is a predilection for both the alcohol and the Ecstasy.

A similar principle applies to dieting. Most eating disorders have deeply psychological roots. Disturb one area of a young life and diet is disturbed. Even a simple suggestion that Sally "should get out more" can turn sour if she gets out to the public house, or if she gets out and doesn't get back till 3am each morning. Maybe the dozens of hours spent engrossed in computers were not mis-spent after all.

Alternative K:
Embracing Religion

Young people could acknowledge a Lord and Saviour. They could return to the faith of their forefathers. If parents are migrants from the New Commonwealth, their English-born children could rediscover the fundamentals of the religion that is their special heritage.

If alcohol is "the dearest idol I have known" (in Cowper's words), then it could be cast off its throne. Teenagers could then worship God alone.

At first sight, religion and alcohol are incompatible. Religion is usually a satisfying experience on its own, the solution- to many of life's difficulties, uncertainties, and absurdities. God reaches the parts other spirits miss.

True enough, thousands of young people do join a church, a chapel or a college Methsoc., or else they go to a church-based youth-club. Thousands do worship with their families, neighbours and friends. They do not just go along for social activities and to take part in fund-raising. Other young people go to special schools at the weekend to learn their scriptures or Hebrew. Many young adherents would not dream of drinking, because it is expressly for-bidden by the elders of their faith — which designates alcohol as sinful. On the other hand, it would be misleading to claim that all migrant children migrate with their faiths. Rejecting religion is sometimes part of rejecting parental norms and aspirations.

Even within the Christian faith, it has been known for a dramatic conversion — a rededication to God, accepting Christ as a personal Saviour — to result in abstinence. In pre-world War One days, the true sign of conversion was teetotalism. Sceptics should hesitate to dismiss the sincere testimony of eager young converts who **have** reformed their drinking habits, and rejected "the demon bottle" forever.

Sadly, the more fervent the conversion the quicker might be the relapse, what religionists call "backsliding". The bottle is more dif-ficult to forsake than initial enthusiasm expected, and the end-product can be a state more dissolute than in the beginning. Also, not all churchgoers, not even all Methodists or Baptists, now have qualms about moderate consumption of alcohol, so a young per-son might turn to God **and** continue drinking.

Summary

Without moving too far into the territory of "solutions", in this chapter it has been possible to glance at alternatives to the drinking of alcohol. Some have been **direct** alternatives like soft drinks, drinking in coffee bars or seeking a deep religious faith. Some have involved **alternative companions** like swots, badminton partners, brides, canoeists and the youth-club set. Others have been **indirect alternatives** that still permit time and space for alcohol intake, but reduce the temptation: the healthy lifestyle, the sporty régime, the diet, an absorbing hobby, a new language to learn.

Quickly one realises that there are remarkably few sure alternatives to alcohol. So often one finds oneself in premises where **other people** are drinking alcohol even when one elects to abstain. It is as if the influence of alcohol on culture and within culture is **already** too pervasive, and therefore irreversible. Drinking is so customary that there are even bars in sports centres and youth conference facilities.

Bold indeed is the parent or teacher, the vicar or the youth-club leader who attempts to **re-direct** teenage drinkers. Such figures will be ridiculed or ignored, told where to go, or told they are out of touch. Once contrasuggestibility is on the cards, many young people will abreact to advice.

Quite different is the position where young people **voluntarily** decide to take up squash, to begin babysitting, or to change their image, or to desert the local inn. Spontaneously, Sally might break an unsuitable engagement, or Samuel might come straight home after playing rugby.

A few alternatives are possible **within** the drinking culture, but modifying it, not attempting to abandon or oppose alcohol outright. Thus pub Pool 8 gives way to the proper snooker hall; Carlsberg gives way to low-alcohol lager; the late night film takes up the part of Saturday evening which would have been spent night-clubbing; a way of life becomes **more** healthy rather than healthiest; or "settling down" reduces the boredom that led in part to drinking. No, alternatives are certainly **not** solutions, but they are slight realignments.

CHAPTER SIX

Discovering the Solution

And may our youthful friends
In this good cause unite,
And bound by sober laws
In Temperance delight —
That soon our nation may be free
From drinking, sin, and misery.

from the Temperance Melodist, 1891.

Is There a Problem

No mileage can be sought or gained finding a "solution" to the phenomenon of teenage drinking if there is no problem. Otherwise commentators and administrators would be put in the position of that famous Permanent Secretary to the Treasury who could find a problem for every solution!

Is teenage drinking, or drinking among young people **a problem**? It is certainly not a classic social problem because alcohol is a socially permitted **and encouraged** substance, More of that later.

Classic social problems either face universal recognition and condemnation, or else a group of respected experts deem there to be a social problem emerging, whereupon they warn the rest of the population. Accepted social problems do not remain static. A change in the law, a shift of public opinion, or the advent of revised attitudes can promote or demote a social problem from where it stood. Some problems graduate to being moral panics; some are relegated to mere social issues; yet more social problems lie dormant.

Parole is a social problem when a prisoner out on licence commits a brutal murder; **absence** of parole is a social problem when prisoners are incited to riot or to burn down cell-blocks. Mods and Rockers are only a social problem so long as they actually exist! Wild, stray or uncontrolled Rottweiler dogs are only a **visible** social problem if there have been a number of recent attacks by such dogs on defenceless children. Surrogacy is a social problem when a woman carries another man's baby for money, but not when she does so for love! Cricket hooliganism is a social problem when supporters run onto the pitch, dig it up and throw bottles at the retreating players, but not when cheerful followers gather noisily round the grandstand to salute the winning team just a few hours later. Unlicensed credit is only a social problem in a society that frowns on debt and on high interest rates; otherwise it is a problem and a misery only for those people without means who are harassed and hounded by backstreet moneylenders.

Social problems are immensely fluid. Basically, they have to be newsworthy and they have to stay in the news. They have to be fairly intractable, like prostitution; or else a new Government edict brushes them aside like Autumn leaves in the wind, as happened when glue sales to young children might have got out of hand.

The best social problems leave no room for argument, or justification, or clarification. Such problems are irreclaimably antisocial. A fine example of a social problem in this category is the passage of speeding juggernauts: overladen 40 ton articulated lorries bearing down on anything in their way, uncontrollably galloping along the nation's highways and by-ways, thundering over pavement edges, brushing alongside the startled occupants of prams and wheelchairs. Ironically, the Ministry of Transport has yet to catch up with speeding juggernauts, so **officially** there is still no problem. Public awareness, the actual experience of something badly wrong, can take a long time to penetrate Whitehall's bureaucratic fortresses.

There can be little disagreement that jerry-building is a social problem, but again it is condoned, even subsidised by central Government. The high Parker-Morris building standards were rejected as too costly.

Commissioning bodies all too rarely inspect workmanship while buildings are being constructed. The LUMP (labour-only-subcontracting) farms out responsibility for shoddy performance to untaxed and uncontactable subcontractors out of the Yellow Pages. Finally, systems-building goes up years before the components all fail in position. Thus, although jerry-building is a problem, society can only get to grips with it by allowing more of it.

However unsatisfactory the conclusion that emerges, it is obvious there is little unanimity as to what is or is not a social problem, and at what stage many isolated incidents come together for public scrutiny as a pervasive nuisance. The letterboxes of 200 immigrant homes might have to be set alight before the Police label racial fire-attacks a social problem. That does not lessen the agony to the first 199 ethnic minority households who needed to move because they caught the attention of arsonists.

The Guardian might see Poverty as a social problem while *The Daily Mail* does not view it as such. Kidneys-for-sale, conversely, might worry *The Daily Mirror* but not *The Independent*. The same **newsagent** who privately condemns perverts, peeping-toms and pimps, might still stock pornographic magazines on his top shelf, the sort of magazines that debase femininity and pander to sexual fantasies.

One way out of the entanglement would be to label an issue as a social problem only when it has victims. On this definition, teenage drinking is not overtly a social problem unless young drinkers **themselves** are counted as victims. Third-party victims are those who get run over or stabbed or knocked over or raided whilst going about their lawful occasions. Crime is drink related, on and off the roads, but related to moderate drinking as well as excessive drinking, related to middle-age drinking as well as to teenage drinking, to the desire for drink as well as the consumption of drink. Strong drink often **exacerbates** crime, and brings it forward; alcohol does not however always **precipitate** crime. In that way, alcohol is vaguely similar to The Broken Home. Divorce and separation are factors in more crimes than marital strife could ever **cause**.

Another way out of the briars would be to define a social problem as that behaviour, or group of activities, which costs the public a great deal of money in taxes and enhances community-charges. Here, as seen in Chapter Two, alcohol scores highly. The conservative calculation of economists is that alcohol, and alcohol damage, costs society £1000 million every year. Net costs to society will feature prominently in the Conclusion.

On balance, it would probably be fair to say that teenage drinking **is** a social problem, although it is not **always** a problem, nor does it always manifest itself in exactly the same way when it is problematic. Youthful drinking is also a **cluster** of behaviours rather than one single form of self-expression. It **does** cost society, and young people themselves, a great deal of money, and more than a few "innocent" victims have their days or their lives ruined.

Just as a nation has a housing stock that soon falls into disrepair if it is not cared for, so a nation has a health stock which will deteriorate and degenerate for wanting of nursing and positive intervention. Part of the total health stock is the health of teenagers. Arguably, that healthiness matters more than the healthiness of older age-groups, as bad health and lack of exercise early on in adulthood store up problems for self and the Health Service many years later. There is no evidence that teenage health has **improved** in the past decade, and alcohol among young people is one of the main reasons for teenage health worsening.

So the public could pay alcohol far more attention. As it is, football hooliganism and hard drugs grab the headlines, although proscribed drugtaking is only one-tenth of the problem of alcohol consumption.

Having established the nature of the problem that must be faced, the solutions to teenage drinking are mutliple and multi-faceted. And with any solution (as with any consequence of alcohol intake) there will come a knock-on effect. To be of most use, one solution might have to lead to another; one Ministry might have to remind another; a tax incentive here might need offsetting against a tax penalty there; policing by consent in one town might only be possible because a neighbouring force has tried confrontational policing.

Piecemeal solutions are totally inadequate. Yet society must patch and darn. It must bring in checks and balances: a little here, a little more there. There can be no "final solution" like Prohibition. If a solution is too daunting and too threatening, the majority of the population, and the majority of magistrates and police personnel who must enforce that solution, will be antipathetic and land up doing nothing, sitting back and hoping the problem will go away, finding the means worse than the end. In that case, teenage drinking will **not** go away; it will simply go on being absorbed into the culture of adult drinking.

The reader can here follow one of ten pathways. Suggested "solutions" are scattered along each of the pathways at irregular intervals. None of the pathways converge, but all cross at different places like dog-runs on a virgin beach. Connections can be made across the sand between the pathways, but such links are not as formal as if a child dug channels in the sand. To stay with the analogy, it could well be that the sea will come in and wash all the pathways away, or wash some away and leave others visible for more tiny feet to emboss. Should the sea of alcohol ever recede far enough then dunes of sense can spring up, and halting pathways in the sand can stabilise to guide wanderers from sea to safety. Some young people will always stay in the sea, or in safety. But because most young people drink, most will need recourse to one or more of these pathways.

1) The Path of Self-Awareness
One modern hymn begins with the first line:

> Let there be Peace on Earth —
> And let it begin with me.

That idea could be extended to the control of alcohol intake, on in many ways that it is just what the Government and the brewers would like to happen: "Let it begin with thee".

That places responsibility for anything that goes right, or wrong, on the individual in view of her **perceived** fecklessness, frivolity, and fallibility, her emotions, her cravings, her weaknesses, her "damaged personality".

The heavy drinker is not coping so the heavy drinker goes under: a social casualty, an irritating statistic. Similarly, the heavy gambler is not coping, and becomes a compulsive gambler. The heavy debtor is not coping and so becomes a bankrupt. The fault is always with **the victim,** inside herself — with the drinker, not with the drink.

That "pathologising" of the problem taken into account, there are still patterns of self-awareness that do allow a young person to manage the consumption of alcohol more harmlessly. One group taking this path called itself DRAMS: Drinking Reasonably and Moderately with Self-control. That about sums it up:

a) Decide When to Start Drinking
Perhaps go to a public house between 7 and 8pm rather than 6 to 9pm. Go to a party from 9 to 10.30pm rather than 8 till Midnight.

b) Decide Whether to Start Drinking
Many young people now decide at the start of their adolescence not to take up smoking. They then keep to that resolution without giving the subject much more thought. Taking less alcohol could find the same response with rather more young people than hitherto, especially if that is a group decision.

c) Decide Upon a Desired Presentation of Self

The decision might be self as charmer, self as athlete, self as wit, self as holy or self as intellectual. Whatever the presentation, the image might limit or reject alcohol.

d) Decide How Much to Drink on Each Occasion

On the way into the inn, fix a drinking quota that will not be exceeded whoever is there with however much money to spare. This quota-setting is popular in drink-drive campaigns. At the disco tonight, make it 2 shandies and a tomato juice. On Valentine's Night for dinner, make it 1½ glasses of medium white wine. At grandmother's house, make it one beaker of her rhubarb-and-turnip brew.

e) Buy Drinks Only for Oneself

This approach gives far more self-control, with an additional measure of self-respect because one depends on no one else.

f) Pace Out Drinking

Hard-Soft-Hard is one pattern. Sherry-soft-soft-soft is another pattern. Hard - hour's wait - Hard - hour's wait - Hard, is a third pattern.

g) Separate Alcohol and Friendship

Say to a friend: "I prefer to buy my own", or, "Can we meet somewhere different from a pub?" Friendship is a nuisance where it imposes an expectation that might not have been there in the first place — for instance, 'I buy you two drinks, then it's up to bed".

h) Develop Polite Ways of Saying No

This is different from making feeble **excuses** like: "I'm losing weight", or "It's doctor's orders". Perhaps say instead: "No thanks, I'm not drinking", or' "That was a kind invitation to your party but one I'm not able to accept", or "I shall not be bringing a bottle, but I shall be bringing two one-litre boxes of fruit juice."

Saying NO is much easier if one's glass is already half-full, and some drinkers keep the same glass half-full for two hours. It is also easier to say NO with a smile. Then partners and acquaintances do not take the huff. You reject the drink, not the drinker.

The Temperance Movement again had a verse for the moment:

There is a little word
Which quickly may be spoken,
Yet many find it hard to say —
And good resolves are broken.

Oh young abstainers listen not
When tempted by the foe —
But in the path of safety keep,
And quickly answer: "NO!"

i) Be Prepared to Insist on No More Drink if Pressed
Insistence might involve greater assertiveness if a companion has not got the message clear the first time: "No more thanks, — REALLY." "I have drunk quite enough for one lunchtime." "I'll say it just once more: NO" No is a curious word because it allows no comeback. It is a complete word which ideally requires no elaboration.

j) Keep a Drinking Diary
Monday September 7th: One sherry at Noon, 2 x ½ cider, 7pm.
Tuesday September 8th: One glass of wine, 1.30pm.
Wednesday September 9th: 4 glasses of lager = 2 pints, 8 to 9.30pm.
It is important to put **every** drink down and to refer back.

k) Chart a Drinking Career
Write a curriculum vitae as if for an employer giving all one's drinking accomplishments next to the year.

l) Making a Drinking Map
Draw a local town or rural district plan marking each drinking place, what beer it sells, and how often it can expect a visit from oneself or other customers. If a different member of the family drinks at a different hostelry, mark that down, too.

m) Making a Drinking Bank-Account
On January 1st each year, start a little cash book. On one side of each page write down the cost of all drinks purchased by self; on the other side of the page, the cost of all drinks bought by parents and friends and hosts for self. Take the cash-book along to the public house every visit.

n) Keeping a Health Diary
This could be written alongside the drinking diary, for example:
Saturday 12th September: Bad hangover after last night's party. Stayed in bed till 11.30am.
Sunday 13th September: I felt very drowsy after lunch. I wish I had not offered to finish up bottle of wine.
Thursday 17th September: I was terribly sick tonight, all over

the bathroom. I wanted such a happy birthday but I kept accepting Rounds.

o) Ask Oneself Questions
Like:
"Does my drinking harm anyone else?" or "Do I need to drink to be myself and to do the things I want to do?" or "Am I influencing someone else to consume alcohol?"

p) Disinvest in Breweries
This is very difficult to do because many large conglomerate companies like The Hanson Trust and Cadbury-Schweppes have diverse interests which might include tobacco, leisure, foods, china, and fashions as well as brewing. It might be a start for a young person to go to a grocery shop without a licence to sell alcohol, or to ask his bank which breweries it advises. Spare savings could be put in an ethical unit trust. A scrapbook could be kept of newscuttings about alcohol, breweries and take-overs. Renewal of a public house licence could be opposed at petty sessions if the publican is misbehaving, selling to under-age drinkers or employing fearsome and unthinking bouncers. Perhaps not buy a book published by a brewery or go to concert sponsored by a brewery. Perhaps stop taking a newspaper that features lager-competitions. Write to the local M.P. to ask whether he speaks or writes on behalf of the licensed trade. Begin and end a ramble at a venue different from a public house.

2) The Path of Parental Intervention
Parents have a responsibility to the young people they brought into the world. Even separation or divorce does not diminish that responsibility, nor justify letting a teenager go anywhere, anytime, without having to give warning, or some account.

Many parents think their children's drinking life is a No-Go area, like their children's smoking life or love-life, but here are some constructive forms of intervention:

- not keeping very much alcohol in the house or on display. Not having cupboards and cabinets filled with full or empty bottles
- not shopping for alcohol in the company of children
- setting a good example of abstinence or light social drinking being aware of young eyes watching closely
- watching television with children to interrupt certain sitcoms

or advertisements; to counteract powerful pro-alcohol messages discussing programmes when they have ended

- asking when and where a teenage party is to be held Who is invited? At what time might the party end?
- discussing a child's friendships in and out of school, later in the workplace, and in leisure time; raising young friends' drinking behaviour as part of general gossip
- insisting on a realistic payment for board and lodgings from the young earner or part-time worker. A contribution towards keep might be requested even if it is not essential to the family's economy
- helping a teenager plan her spending, so that she has money left over for tights, toothpaste, magazines and petrol; so that The Duke William does not take it all
- commenting if a teenager, or his friend, smells of alcohol, or wanders in tipsy
- making a No Drinking and Driving rule as the precondition for teaching a son or daughter how to drive, or financing a first car or motorcycle. That rule could apply to the family car — whoever drives it. Without an undertaking, even lifts to the public house or to parties and dances could be refused
- emphasising that there is no such thing as a free drink, even when on holiday
- stressing alternatives to alcohol and alternatives to alcohol-focussed leisure pursuits
- showing quiet concern when a child's drinking habit is obviously moving towards excess; retelling one's own drinking career and past drinking problems; pointing out that a current level of alcohol consumption is unacceptable and unmaintainable
- allowing no drunkenness in the marriage or the home
- not emphasising the activity of home brewing; using home-brewed drinks sparingly.

One task most parents cannot undertake is the educational **lecture.** If the explicit lesson comes from a parent's lips, that is sufficient incentive for many a teenager to go and do the opposite!

3) The Path of General Practitioner Guidance

The GP is in a very good position to detect a growing drink problem in a young patient. The practice might have known a teenager since birth. When later that person presents herself, perhaps with symptoms not immediately associated with alcohol, the G.P. can ask sensitively about the place of alcohol in her life. WHO — the World Health Organization — produces a screening instrument, and the book: *"Alcohol Problems"* (by Anderson, Wallace & Jones) was written with G.P.s in mind, and gives many other leads.

Some family doctors do themselves have a drink problem, and may be less alert to incipient difficulties in their patients' lives. Additionally, they may only have an average of 3½ minutes to give to each person in the waiting-room. Nevertheless, diarrhoea, nerves, migraine, insomnia, depression or lumbago might have an alcoholic origin and the most hard-pressed G.P. could ask further questions or seek a second opinion.

It is incumbent upon the whole medical profession to begin to discard the term "drug" in favour of "harmful substance", and to reject "alcoholism" in favour of "drinking problem". The whole concept of "alcoholism" needs redefining (but not here) because:

- alcoholism sounds like a disease, not a symptom
- the word "disease" has no exact parallel with problem drinking
- alcoholism is traditionally **the most extreme** consequence of alcohol dependence. So extreme is it that many problem-drinkers believe they have escaped the hazard by not being called Alcoholic
- alcoholism grabs the headlines to the detriment of lesser drink problems
- alcoholism as a disease allows the (unattainable) prospect of **a cure**
- alcoholism conjures up a scruffy-tramp-on-a-park-bench image, that takes no account of respectable heavy drinkers
- alcoholism makes incipient heavy drinkers sure that adjustments are not needed **yet**
- alcoholism further deceives the heavy drinker into believing he has a **better** self, or true self, that is not greedy, ambitious, unkind, thoughtless, unimaginative or insensitive, **if only** he could give up alcohol (so that on that Golden Horizon of abstinence, the grand new self could step out, cleansed and instantly likeable.) Two selves do not in fact exist, and **both** selves can be a disappointment.

4) The Path of Social Work Support

Social workers have usually been reluctant to intervene when alcohol has been a factor in the lives of families brought to their notice, **even where** alcohol led directly or indirectly to a child coming into Care. It is estimated that 40% of all social services' referrals are alcohol-linked and that 20% of all patients admitted to psychiatric hospital on a social worker's recommendation have a serious drink problem as well. The reticence of social workers can be put down to:

- social workers' own consumption of alcohol (generally quite heavy)
- a dislike of delving into the inner workings of some families
- non-judgment as a fundamental tenet in counselling
- a particular unwillingness to "lecture" young people under supervision
- an unwavering belief that it is up to an individual or a family how they spend their own income
- a sympathy for poor and downtrodden families whose only real escape from drudgery and unemployment is beer and cigarettes
- a learned helplessness with alcohol counselling
- certainty that alcohol is really **a medical** issue, the province of the medical world, best left to GPs and medics
- time constraints, putting problem drinking low down on the list of social work priorities
- reluctance to address the concurrent problems of vagrancy and homelessness
- a belief that drink has already gone down too far before help is requested
- problem drinking is a very private phenomenon, unlikely to be referred
- a benign attitude towards the difficulties of drinking in the elderly population. Only home helps visit many elderly people. Should we stop somebody drinking himself to death?

This reticence understood, there are still many ways many social workers and probation offficers can help problem young drinkers:

- making up a drinking diary as part of supervision
- facilitating a self-help group (perhaps as part of Intermediate Treatment for repeat offenders)
- offering young offenders a six-week alcohol project as part of a deferred sentence, where the original offence was drink-induced (such a scheme operates successfully in Tayside)
- offering counselling or attendance at a special unit as a direct alternative to prison
- offering retraining sessions and driving skills lessons for young people arrested on drink-drive charges (such a scheme for adults

was pioneered by a probation officer in Hampshire)

- raising the subject of alcohol during home visits and counselling sessions
- never meeting, or responding to, referrals in a public house
- not befriending a new young supervisee in a public house
- not leaving a case conference without raising the question of the impact of alcohol on an emergency or an instance of cruelty
- offering paid and unpaid carers support in their task of nursing or attending to people whose lives are being disrupted by alcohol
- training volunteers to spend time with young drinkers
- enabling young people to change their drinking repertoire and so to alter the course of their young drinking careers
- giving children in a household support when a parent has a severe drinking problem
- asking prospective adopters and fostercarers about their drinking routines, and the importance of alcohol to them
- not turning a blind eye to drunkenness or repeat drinking when it affects the residents — or staff — of children's homes, probation hostels or family centres
- giving families help-line numbers they can use when alcohol emerges as a problem
- giving talks in schools about social problems resulting from excessive intake of alcohol, and liaising with schools about teenagers whose work and attendance is falling off through alcohol
- not colluding with parents in labelling one young family member the "bad client", or "the fountain of all the family's ills"
- encouraging young people to take some responsibility for their own drinking behaviour, not blaming friends, or the pub, or colleagues
- not allowing young drinkers to get away with excuses about celebration or: "The doctor knows, and will cure it"
- obtaining and showing films about alcohol
- setting respondents a clear drinking-target, and meeting them each week to lower it, or to re-negotiate, the target
- setting young people a good example by not drinking when away on camp, between visits, or at lunchtime on work-days.

5) The Path of Employer Intervention

Very many employers are now intervening where they suspect that performance or absenteeism is being affected by alcohol. Employers used to have a quiet word in the ear of the new recruit or chargehand or department head. Or else they used the sack, dismissing drinkers drinking at or before work. Some employers did not want to admit the high correlation between industrial mishaps and accidents and drink, nor did they want the organisation to get a bad name.

Some employers like Royal Mail and British Rail have employed external consultants who work with their personnel departments to identify and to assist problem drinkers before dismissal is even considered as an option. The best counsellors are completely independent. They look for the employee who has every Monday off, or who suffers many minor ailments that might not normally justify absence.

So worried were advertisers about the pressures on young marketing executives, many of whom were suffering from stress, tension, drug-abuse, and indebtedness, as well as from heavy drinking, that they asked the National Advertising Benevolent Society to set up an employee Help-Line which currently receives 35 calls each week. An associated J. Walter Thompson advertising campaign in the marketing trade press uses all the skills of advertising copywriters to outline the triple problems of stress, drink and forced unemployment. Even the boy outside Selfridges wearing a sandwich-board is included as "at risk". And employers soon benefit from intervention.

6) The Path of Initiatives from the Drinks Industry

Despite the limitations (and anomalies) of the present licensing laws there is far more that the drinks industry could do to clean up its image and to help young drinkers. There is an old saying: "Dead customers ring no tills". It is no use a firework factory producing fireworks and disregarding the question how fireworks will be sold and let off. Similarly, brewers have to think how their products will be sold and let in. The whole drinks' industry includes not only the brewers, but manufacturers of soft drinks who supply public houses, supermarket managers, off-licensees, wine bottlers, wine wholesalers, night clubs, licensed hotels, outside caterers, brewery financial consultants, and alcohol carriers. Where can they begin?

- publicans could refuse to serve some young people
- publicans could send their bar staff away on special customer-relations courses that would include meeting teenage drinkers
- publicans could refuse to serve some young drivers and motorcyclists
- they could put up more prominent notices above their bars ex-

plaining why young people might not be served, or might be questioned

- publicans could open really attractive family-rooms and teenage discos, so that 14-19 year olds can sit in comfortable surroundings with plenty of magazines, snacks and soft drinks to hand, perhaps with a lone guitarist or jazz pianist or folk-group to entertain
- bar staff could point out when one or more of a young crowd of drinkers has had enough
- bar staff could also tell customers that they stock many very low-alcohol beers and wines
- hoteliers could think again about minibars in each bedroom
- the price of soft drinks in public bars and restaurants could be reduced to cost-price plus 10%
- more bars could be opened with the separate intention of serving main meals or courses
- public houses could locate some of their quizzes, card-tables, and pool-tables in separate annexes
- bouncers could go away for special training including techniques of non-aggression
- "happy hours" could be abandoned
- the token system could be abandoned where a young drinker gets a "free" prize or holiday, or a competition entry, for collecting most tokens, one token for every ½ pint of lager drunk
- publicans could **ask** local police personnel to visit their premises as part of the duty roster, so that they mix with customers, become known by customers, and can be seen as law-enforcers (Brighton's Police are especially vigilant)
- reputable publicans could ask their local branch of L.V.A. to act against tenants who break the law and who bring the trade into disrepute
- the L.V.A. could run special residential weekends for young people being brought up on licensed premises
- other courses could be run for publicans on how to identify problem drinking among their own young bar staff
- bar staff could be asked not to drink on duty nor to accept free drinks from customers
- publicans could stamp out blatant sexism and racism in their bars
- those hotels and public houses with a beer garden could ask special volunteers to circulate among young drinkers and picnickers

- bars and hotels could discourage drinking competitions, illegal sweepstakes and the silent undercover auction of stolen goods
- a deposit could be charged on glasses to minimise the risk that they will later be hurled at other drinkers
- some unlicensed hotels and caravan sites could be set up to give young holidaymakers a choice
- off licences and supermarkets could check that none of their young employees are stacking, pricing and checking out alcohol
- all shops could ask more questions of young people buying alcohol
- alcoholic beverages could be sold separately not in large boxes or packs of three or six (which is really inertia selling)
- retail drinks could all be unit-priced by the litre so that young shoppers can accurately compare prices and values
- caterers could offer young engaged couples the option of a dry wedding, or one where non-alcoholic wines are poured
- food firms could mark all their packages with the name of the real manufacturer so that young people do not unconsciously support a brewer when they eat, or shop for relatives
- no tee-shirts, badges and special merchandise should advertise alcoholic products, because such leisurewear is worn and seen by millions of young people
- coach companies could refuse to run booze-and-grab day trips to the duty-free ports of the far side of the Channel
- efforts could be-made not to sponsor successful sports' clubs and teams which young people identify with. In 1988 a brewery tie-up with Liverpool Football Club Supporters was mooted, but later dropped.

7) The Path of Lobbying

Lobbying is an important twentieth Century activity. It covers "planting" news stories where they will get published, waylaying MPs, writing to ministers, organising a stunt which will be reported, commissioning surveys, forming Pressure Groups, running one-issue campaigns, speaking in schools and youth-clubs, and seeking influence in all high places. Lobbyists in the United States have perfected the activity, but there are some good British examples of public-awareness campaigns.

Although lobbying has never been healthier (or unhealthier, if one dislikes decision-making behind closed doors), alcohol-concern lobbying has never been in a poorer state. The lobby as a whole is weak, demoralised, fragmented, underfunded, directionless, inward-looking, confused and in competition with itself rather than with the powerful drinks industry.

Many bodies are doing the same thing separately or separate things in the same way. Additionally, some parts of the alcohol-concern lobby are unsure whether their aim is light drinking, moderate drinking, restrained drinking, opposition-to-Alcoholism, temperance, teetotallism, or **militant** teetotallism or simply the expression of concern about alcohol in society. I do not call this lobby "the anti-alcohol lobby", because that is an unhelpful and negative title. The lobby can see some good in the light drinking of alcohol with self-awareness. So alcohol-concern is a neutral title, not to be confused with the organisation called ALCOHOL CONCERN.

To illustrate the problem of this lobby, here is a list of some of the organisations — some now defunct — whose literature and ideas I used when writing this book:

Alcohol Concern
Alcohol Concern (Wales)
National Council on Alcoholism
ACCEPT
Scottish Council of Alcoholism
The Alcohol Education Centre
DAWN
Royal College of Physicians
World Health Organisation
N.A.C.R.O.
Alcoholics Anonymous
The Alcohol Forum
The Alcohol Counselling Service
Action on Alcohol Abuse
The Alcohol Education & Research Council
U.K. Temperance Alliance
Drinkwatchers
Royal College of Psychiatrists
Health Education Council
The Centre for Alcohol Studies
Alcohol Problems Advisory Service
British Medical Association
F.A.R.E.
Federation of Local Alcohol Groups
The Institute of Alcohol Studies

Medical Council on Alcoholism
The Independent Order of the Rechabites

The duplication and disarray affecting the alcohol-concern lobby stands in sharp contrast to the supremacy of A.S.H. — Action on Smoking and Health — in the field of tobacco-concern. But the splintering is inevitable when these factors are considered:

- alcohol is a very popular substance
- a very large proportion of the population aged 15 and over drink — and enjoy — alcoholic beverages
- there is no discernable tide of opinion running behind more restrictive views and laws on alcohol
- teetotallism is a prerequisite for joining certain Temperance groups
- teetotallers are traditionally suspicious of light drinkers and vice-versa
- the mass media are broadly pro-alcohol and rely on alcohol advertising
- the discussion of alcoholism overshadows all other alcohol issues, and solutions to alcoholism are not the same as for other drinking patterns
- some alcohol-concern groups appear joyless and self-righteous
- other alcohol-concern groups appear intent on destroying the liberty of the individual and his right to self-determination
- alcohol as a subject may have become too medicalised for non-medical opinions to be represented.
- only £1 is spent on alcohol-concern for every £300 spent on alcohol promotion
- everytime the dangers of alcohol are outlined, the price of alcoholic beverages actually **falls** in real terms
- brewers cunningly actually **fund** some alcohol concern-work and research into alcoholism, leading the lobby to a loss of independence
- the Brewers' Lobby is very powerful and well-respected
- the alcohol-concern lobby is not sure whether to run hostels and rehabilitation units directly or to concentrate on campaigning and coordination
- alcohol problems have been **personalised** in the past: "If every drinker was responsible, there would be no alcohol concern."

8) The Path of Advertising Restrictions

Brewers and distillers spend at least £200 million each year on the direct advertising of their products or on sponsorship.

In 1959 — the time of the famous Guinness Poster: See what You Can Do: — only £15m. was spent on advertising and by 1969 the figure had only risen to £51m., so growth has been strong recently, roughly in line with increased consumption.

Currently, whisky and spirits cannot be advertised on TV at all, and advertising of beer and lager is discouraged during children's programming. Other points of note in the I.B.A. Code (which covers I.T.V. and Channel 4, not magazines and newspapers — which are also seeing an upsurge in very lucrative alcohol advertising especially in weekend colour supplements) are that:

- advertizers must not use famous sports' personalities for promotion
- they must not show close-to drinking by under-25 year olds
- they must not imply that drinking alcohol leads to sexual success
- they must not use subliminal persuasion
- they must be aware of their "social responsibility"
- they must not use humour to subvert the intention of other regulations and restrictions.

How well TV advertisers live up to their responsibility can be seen in Appendix Two, which comments on certain advertisements for alcoholic beverages shown in 1989.

Even the briefest evening by the television shows that most alcohol adverts **are** humorous, amongst the funniest of all adverts, and that they do use a variety of video techniques, and that they do show youngish drinkers in preference to the doddering inmates of a local elderly persons' home. Also the advertisements **do** underline the way that the drinker who drinks most makes most friends.

When interviewers from Strathclyde University asked 433 Glaswegian secondary school pupils, they found that alcohol advertising has a profound impact on this age-group. Some of the sample had picked up the brewers' messages before the age of ten! One teenager said that lagers were drunk by sophisticated young people. Another commented: "Beer is for the macho type of man who gets all the girls". All the respondents pointed out their identification with the central characters of the advertisements, many of whom were glamorous and sun-burnt.

There was an 86% pupil approval for the adverts that were screened to the strains of two pop songs: "You've got the Power", and "One Great Thing". Moreover, when schoolchildren were shown 9 still photographs from beer adverts, two-thirds of the sample instantly recognized 4 stills or more **and** matched them with a brand correctly.

In 1989, advertising agent Leo Burnett was given the Gordon's Gin account with the brief to make gin-drinking more popular among young people, thus shedding the colonial fuddy-duddy image. What Burnett came up with was a series of advertisements showing nothing but a flat green background. Beneath each advert were a few words that could have come from a cheap Christmas cracker: "A snowman drinking a G. & T. in June", "A Martian sloshing through mushy peas", or "A snooker table with no balls and no tonic". Burnett (and Gordon) wanted young people to desert Bacardi and vodka and drink more gin. They also wanted to present the colour green very positively in the Green Year of Conservation, as many young people marched to the Green banner. Gordon's already has its imitators: flattery if not hilarity.

Advertisers defend themselves by saying that they only advertise in order to keep their products in the public eye, and that advertising does not increase the market for alcohol, rather it encourages drinkers to switch from one brand to another. They also say that Scotch whisky sales have doubled in the time they have **not** been advertised on television.

This defence is not altogether convincing because no one except soon-to-be-privatised businesses would advertise just to keep their name alive, and the brewers want a realistic return for their investment — it often costs as much as half a million pounds just to **film** a screen advert. Also no new lager would be bottled unless accompanied by persistent and aggressive advertising, so there must be a market, and marketing opportunities, for new lagers.

The brand-switching argument also lacks conviction because only alcohol and tobacco advertisers use it; they only use it publicly, not privately; and they only argue using industry survey data, not independent research data.

Regarding background music, when the manager of Tennents was challenged about his firm's use of teenage pop-tracks to make Tennents' lagers stay uppermost in young minds, he retorted: "What do you want me to do? Shut off the television?"

The Director of the Brewers' Society, Sir Edgar Sanders, hit the nail on the head when he addressed a conference with these words:

"If we can once attract a new class of customer, we shall see the brewery trade turn round and start the ascending scale. I am not saying that the present beer drinker should drink more but rather that we want new customers. We want to get the beer-drinking habit instilled into thousands, almost millions, of young men who do not at present know the taste of beer. These young men, if they start with what they can afford today, as they grow up will afford better beer to the greater advantage of the brewing industry". Those words are over half a century old but their content has never been ignored by the rampant brewing industry, now **very much** in the ascendancy.

One very simple solution would be to ban alcohol advertising altogether on television, and later in magazines. The only possible drawback here is that when cigarette advertising was removed from television screens, thousands of young people believed cigarettes were still being advertised in between ITV programmes because of the prevailing tobacco **culture.**

Local authorities own many prominent advertising sites in towns and cities, and near to public buildings. Local authorities could restrict poster-advertising by making more conditions on the use of their own sites. Already, alcohol and tobacco are not advertised in Kent schools although that county encourages other hoardings in their playgrounds. It cannot be long before lessons, textbooks, exercise books and school equipment are used to carry advertisements or sponsorship. Brewers may yet get into schools by the back door, starting with the new city technology colleges.

In any discussion of the advertising of alcohol, **public relations** should not be forgotten. The world of public relations, general lobbying, and company promotion — as well as the world of company recruitment and corporate identity — relies heavily on the skills of public relations' executives with their leaflets, glossy magazines, promotional videos, lectures, luncheons, receptions and news briefings. Nearly all these occasions, including not a few charity spectaculars, swim in alcohol. Mini-skirted waitresses circulate P.R. functions with readily refillable glasses of wine and sherry. Young workers are introduced to P.R. at the very start of their careers when various government job-creation and enterprise schemes are "sold" to them. Young people should see that alcohol is not the natural beginning of public image making.

9) The Path of Portraying Alcohol Less on Television and Radio

Alcohol actually gets itself advertised free of charge on many programmes other than advertising breaks, and in numerous radio plays:

- the public house is used as a focus of activity
- drama begins in a public house like The Bull (in The Archers) or The Rover's Return (in Coronation Street).
- comedians joke about drunkenness
- gin and whisky are used to move the dialogue along
- there is an invitation to all on the screen to join in a glass of wine or sherry
- there are constant reminders of the home drinks' cabinet (especially in "Terry and June")
- men enter the drama afresh by coming in from the Local,
- alcohol is served before and during company board-meetings
- there are shots of decanters on ledges or sideboards
- young people come in from leisure pursuits and then go off to the pub or the club
- documentaries are filmed against a background of frothing beer
- young people stand round their sporting heroes who then open an enormous bottle of champagne and hold it beside their groins.

One detailed study by Anders Hansen: "The Portrayal of Alcohol on Television", makes fascinating reading. Hundreds of programmes were watched with a score given to every setting where alcohol was portrayed and every scene where actors and actresses were actually filmed drinking alcohol. 87% of all fiction programmes had some reference to alcohol, and 72% showed characters consuming alcohol. Alcohol was portrayed in a surprising half of all **non-fictional programmes**, with 11% of such programmes showing personalities drinking alcohol in front of the cameras.

There were 1.6 alcohol scenes per hour in non-fiction programmes and 3.4 references per hour in fictional programmes, 3 of these actually filming the drinker drinking. The many celebrations happening in television programmes could be seen as justifying more alcohol on the screen. Many firms of all description pay companies and movie-film directors to **place** their products somewhere on view.

Conversely, Hansen found, there were few if any references to **alcohol abuse**, or the link of alcohol with homicide, suicide, marital strain, cars crashing and ill-health. Usually when alcohol *is* shown in a negative light on TV, it is the **false** lead to distract detectives. Thus its influence is toned down. 138 programmes were viewed; in only 3 did an "alcoholic" appear as a story-line — a sick person under pressure, conforming to the stereotype. Ironically, "Howard's Way", a soap opera about the affluent gin-and-tonic boating set, did give some prominence to a boatyard owner with a serious drinking problem. The impact of his decline and fall would have been much starker if the rest of the cast had not been always drinking!

Situation comedies treat consumption of alcohol — particularly consumption by women or young adults — as great fun. One-sixth of the actors drinking on sitcoms appear to be under-age. Half are upper-middle-class, and less than 5% are dossing or living in destitution whilst they are filmed drinking. One in eight actors drinks in the screen workplace! Fewer than one in 25 drinks all alone.

On television, women drink wine; men drink beer. The macho image of the heavy and repetitive drinker is never questioned — indeed, the standard portrayal is confirmed as normal. Nor are the portrayed links between alcohol and questionable business deals ever brought under scrutiny. American films show 2 people drinking at home for every one drinking in public; English dramas and documentaries show one person drinking at home for every 2 in a public place.

TV producers and radio script-writers defend their portrayal of alcohol by saying that they are only showing what happens in real life. Alcohol is such a prominent subject that they claim they would be negligent limiting its appearance on the almost-universally owned receiving sets. They go on to suggest that excluding alcohol would give it cult status, as a forbidden substance to be consumed secretly. Further, they say that when they are televising major sporting occasions, they have no say in the perimeter advertising which just happens to come into focus.

10) The Path of Changes in the Licensing Laws

This is a very tricky and thorny issue for any Government short of Parliamentary time, or even private members' time. Moral issues like raising or lowering the Age of Consent always carry lower priority than economic measures like taxation, the financing of the Health Service and the topping up of student loans.

As with the age of consent, the age of drinking in public is bound to be arbitrary. Arguably a married woman of 17 should be able to buy a Martini in a public house. Equally, it is wrong that she can be almost forced to have sexual intercourse **although** she is now over the age of 16.

One obvious change in the Licensing laws would be to forbid any bar or club or public house or special function to have an extension of licence after the hours of 11am to 11pm. Monday to Saturday.

Another change would be to give J.P.s the power to shut down any pub where under 16 year olds have been served at the bar with alcohol. A token, and effective, shut-down would be for 2 weeks. A public house could also be shut down for four weeks if there had been a fight or scuffle involving young drinkers.

Publicans could be told that adults **must** accompany their children in children's rooms annexed to public houses. Unaccompanied children are allowed to roam free at present. Gambling machines could be banned from public houses, as these often attract teenagers.

Furthermore, public house car parks could be dug up, because **any** drinking and driving brings added danger. In order to be served, car drivers should have to wear a special DRIVER badge like coach operators already supply to their PSV drivers.

Licensing hours could be staggered so that one public house clears its bar half an hour before its competitor, on a rotating basis. Drinking-up time could be scrapped and Rounds could be forbidden after 8pm.

If the age for drinking on licensed premises was reduced to 16, that would be more consistent with the lower onset of puberty, and earlier maturity, also with the time of leaving school. As it is, thousands of 16 and 17 year olds being served with alcoholic beverages without fuss brings the law into disrepute. During the 1980s, prosecutions for underage drinking have dropped from 4000 per year to about 700, with some cities and counties reporting no prosecutions at all! That situation could make an already unenforceable law laughable.

On the other hand, if the age for being served in a supermarket or public house was raised to 20, that would emphasize that drinking alcohol in teenage years is **never** entirely safe. Or such a message could be put on every bottle and every can of alcohol.

The most realistic change in law could be a requirement that every young drinker should carry an identity card, perhaps photograph, date of birth and National Insurance number. Such cards would help bar staff and check-out staff and would save embarrassing confrontations with the police or publicans. But there are civil liberties' issues. Identity cards (tried with success in at least one town as an L.V.A. experiment) do remind people of war, of South African passes, and of the discredited notion of a football-supporter identity card system.

Despite reservations, the Portman Group announced in October 1989 a "proof-of-age" card, a card to be tried by Britain's eight largest breweries during the early 1990s. The card will be compulsory for young drinkers in most public houses and will be actively promoted to supermarket chains. The Portman Group is a brewers' body fronted by a credible educationist Dr. John Rae. It professes to be worried about a "media obsession with lager louts".

Another change in the licensing law could require supermarkets and off-licences to have a separate alcohol annexe. Garages, video shops and sports' centres could be prohibited altogether from selling alcoholic beverages. Off-licences could be restricted in number to one for every 3000 of population, or every village, whichever is smaller. Licensing could be transferred from the magistracy to local government, with fewer loopholes.

The 1988 Licensing Act which freed bars to open longer could be reviewed with the possibility of cutting out teatime drinking, and late-morning drinking. Nor have longer opening hours led to drinkers spreading out the same drink throughout a drinking session, ending the last-minute rush. Scotland may not even have been the best model to use for the 1988 "liberalisation".

Finally, some action is possible to reduce the ridiculously high prices of soft drinks behind the bar. Perhaps no bar should charge for orange **squash**, and every bar should have a full range of soft drinks costing 30 pence or less. Had the Monopolies and Mergers' Commission recommendations found favour, fewer inns would have been tied to breweries and their subsidiary soft-drink bottling plants.

A very full discussion of all aspects of Licensing Law reform is included in the Home Office Report: "Young People and Alcohol". Many of the working group's recommendations have yet to be implemented.

*   *   *

The Government's Own Choice: The Path of Health Education

The proposition is simple. Educate all young people about the dangers of alcohol consumption. Pay a public body or an advertising firm to coordinate such education. Encourage more mass media attention to health education initiatives. Follow up films and discussions every few months. Use outside speakers. End of problem.

If health education is the preferred solution, there is absolutely no difficulty identifying places where this education can happen. First use secondary schools with their almost 100% captive audience. Use school assemblies, personal and social education classes, even games' lessons on wet days. Use the audiovisual equipment already installed in schools. Follow receptive young people into their youth clubs. Put up posters in doctors' surgeries and on the noticeboards of leisure centres. Pursue the notion of captive audience to television programmes and public service advertising slots so that the health education message is reinforced. Print pamphlets and study-packs to accompany broadcasts. Occasionally put a leaflet through every teenager's letter-box. "A partnership for change". "Drink Sensibly. Eat Sensibly."

The Advantages of Health Education Addressing Alcohol Issues:

Health Education must have many advantages because it is now so well tried and tested in related fields like smoking, AIDS, and the need for exercise. There was even the beginning of a sugary and fatty foods campaign. Such campaigns build on previous expertise, and use all the methods of commercial promotions to counteract the competing messages of other interest-groups.

There is some evidence that children **do** take note of some warnings in school because they carry the authority of educators who are not misleading in other rôles, or in the science lab. Most young people now know that smoking damages health and that eggs should be well cooked and that tartzatrine leads to hyperactivity in children. Some health slogans like "Clunk-Click", and "Drinka Pinta Milka Day!" became catch-phrases in their own right.

Teenagers do read youth club notice-boards and they do study magazines like LIVING, JUST 17 and BELLA for hours, so they have not become hardened cynics repelling messages. Teenagers like fads, and spot a new scare from afar. Early indication from the SAY NO TO STRANGERS campaign and from sexual abuse videos in the classroom point to young people's wariness of intimacy with adults who cannot be trusted. Teenagers are curious, and certainly A.I.D.S. propaganda harnessed that curiosity. Some teenagers share a fund of goodwill which responds generously to disasters and disabilities, which raises large sums of money for charity, and which lectures grown-ups to be more sensitive to environmental issues!

Health Education has another advantage. It is amazingly neutral. It is **supposed** to be uncontroversial and apolitical — to inform, not to upset. At the same time, it is planned in such a way that the communicators, the mediators of the message, such as teachers, doctors and parents are not **themselves** anxious about their missionary task.

Health itself is rather a neutral area. Everyone wants good health, and more of it. The Readers' Digest sells well because it is hooked on health. Family Circle has found a similar fascination amongst its readers. Already it has been noted that alcohol-concern has been reduced by medical interests to health-concern, so health education is a natural start and finishing point.

Moreover, health education is remarkably cheap, cheaper than any of the alternative paths towards solving teenage drinking problems. Television stations can be persuaded to broadcast a documentary free-of-charge to the Government, and teachers would be employed in schools in any case. Then if young people do not imbibe the message, that is their own fault. They were given it clearly and often, and they should know better.

The Disadvantages of Health Education Addressing Alcohol Issues

Again, some of the negative points raised in one health campaign apply to **all** such campaigns. Messages can be muddled and mishandled. Then you get doctors and educators arguing with each other in public. Messages can also be naïve and unhelpful. Posters, leaflets, and full-page newspaper ads concerning AIDS were very contentious.

There are the twin risks of oversaturation and over-kill. Too many posters and messages and you get a mass turn-off: "not **another** report on smoking and lung disease". Charities have discovered something they call "compassion fatigue", when benefactors look the other way. Overkill is where a health education campaign makes its message so horrific with so many scary photographs and frightening images, and line upon line of snappy injunctions, that teenagers are actually directed **toward** the hazard they are supposed to be avoiding. The mystery and romance are greater if **everybody** disapproves, especially if every parent is alarmed.

More subtly, sometimes a message is locked in the classroom and cannot get out. The lesson is excellent: rehearsed, discussed, documented, agreed with. The lesson ends and the message lapses. This phenomenon is seen best with so-called football hooliganism. All those lessons on violence are forgotten in the heat and excitement of the match viewed from behind goal.

There is also an age-old debate as to whether health education campaigns have measurable results. Contaminating factors get in between cause and result. Health campaigners say that one of their chief objectives is to raise public awareness ready for a change of law. The first seat-belt campaign definitely did **not** get every driver and front-seat passenger belting up, but it did make it easier for Parliament to make the wearing of seat-belts compulsory with less of an outcry. The public probably needs a clear law in some instances. "Softening-up" is also used in commercial advertizing, and in the unattributed briefings of Downing Street spokesmen.

Alcohol-awareness may suffer if the health education campaign is not as forceful as the brewers' campaign, or if young people smoke more to make up for not drinking. Alcohol-awareness also reaches rock bottom when teenagers hear a huge hard-drugs horror story and find that alcohol is not included among harmful substances! The most recent drugs campaign, launched in June 1989 does include alcohol, and for years doctors and police visiting certain schools have been requested explicitly to include alcohol as one of the "drugs" under discussion. As one parent put it: "What is the point of teaching about drugs our children do **not** take whilst ignoring the drugs they **do** take?"

The Government has also been confused in telling people alcohol can do harm, at the same time increasing its supply, cheapness, and accessibility. All health messages must converge or else inconsistency is the only message. The Government got into its worst muddle with healthy-eating. Research findings were suppressed; leaflets were printed then not distributed; Government-funded scientists were dismissed; leaflets that were available were not promoted; the Ministry of Agriculture, Fisheries and Foods fell out with the Ministry of Health; in the end The Health Education Council itself was abolished! — all so that children should not desert sugary and fatty foods (foods they might not even know are detrimental to their health) in favour of foods full of fibre, vitamins and useful carbohydrates.

There was also controversy surrounding an E.E.C. proposal for the labelling of cigarette packets. Britain was not prepared to acquiesce to a Brussels' directive, and the issue remains unresolved despite a dozen or so messages being possible on a small cigarette packet, each deserving not to be overlooked. That does not augur well for Britain emulating the United States and printing warnings on bottles: "Alcohol Endangers Health", or "Pregnant Women should not Drink".

Nor is there an easy way of stressing **which** drinks are most harmful. The Unit or the Standard Drink have been excellent tools of measurement, but less than a third of young people understand the equation: ½ pint of beer = 1 glass of table wine = one measure of whisky, ten years after the equation was first adopted to replace the more difficult percentage volume of alcohol still printed on wine and spirits bottles.

Future health education campaigns must broaden the message that alcohol could lead to bad health; it also harms young people's wealth, their sobriety, their standing in the community, their sense of direction, their relationships and their work performance. That broader message would still have to compete with the new CRACK campaign, and a veritable warfare between Welsh, Australian and Scottish lager-brewers who pretend to challenge each other in the market-place in no kinder a manner than rival Italian ice-cream salesmen.

Summary

This chapter has moved outwards from the suggestion that, on the strength of available evidence, teenage drinking **is** a problem, and one that needs addressing. That does not mean that there are "solutions", even less, that there are simple, straightforward, and cheap solutions. Most paths towards a solution are blocked by obstacles and pass through bandit territory.

Some headway can be made by self and self-awareness, by changes in the drinker, not the drink. Parents and general practitioners can advise young people in sensible drinking, and there are many useful social work initiatives where a family becomes known to Social Services. Employers can do much merely by **noticing** the alcohol intake of their young employees, and its effect.

On a broader front, the brewing, catering and allied leisure trades have it within their power to restrict heavy alcohol consumption in all age-groups, partly through training their staff, to guide young customers. Unfortunately, bar staff are also young themselves, and alcohol is at its most comfortable and comforting in its natural habitat. The alcohol-concern lobby could also help, but that lobby stands divided and demoralised.

Less in the doldrums, advertisers could and should re-examine their alcohol advertisements and even reconsider advertising alcohol at all. Alcohol adverts are certainly humorous and persuasive. The advertisers are supported by programme makers and producers who give alcohol generous, and uncritical, coverage in many ordinary plays, sitcoms and documentaries.

The Government could revise or tighten existing licensing laws which are neither strict nor enforceable at present. However, the Government's most favoured solution is Health Education. A good alcohol-awareness campaign is possible, but unlikely, because all such consciousness-raising initiatives are subject to confusion and diminishing returns.

CONCLUSION

Will Temperance workers now in doubt
About the thing to do,
Allow a word in song to trace
The course we should pursue?
Don't wait till the drunkard is made!
Prevention is better than cure;
A government willing to aid
Is what we must work to secure.

from the Temperance Melodist, 1891

The Government cannot move faster than public consent dictates. Even the most resolute government must listen to voiced opinion and to the press. All governments seek the views of expert witnesses and academics, and respond to the arguments of special interest groups which can also boast scientific respectability.

Capital punishment is a perfect example of where a government must wait till enough people agree with a vote in Parliament. Still a majority of the British public possibly want hanging for certain offences, hanging in theory if not in practice. But arguments against hold sway and gradually gain support.

Alcohol is a very difficult subject on which to legislate or alter the public's perception. There is ample evidence that the consumption of alcohol rises and falls according to price. Petrol, cigarettes and ice-cream are similarly price-sensitive. If beer was available at 5 pence a pint, there would be unimaginable consumption and consequences! Conversely, if the price was five **pounds** a pint, there would be greatly reduced consumption, and a reduction in alcohol-related illnesses and problems.

When in 1981 the price of alcohol rose higher than the inflation for the first time in 30 years, there was a temporary drop in consumption. Alcohol drinkers **could** be penalised to the extent where they dropped their empty glasses on the bar counter and fled.

Alcoholic beverages would now need to be priced 40% higher just to regain their 1977 position in the range of consumer options, pound for pound.

No government will, however, contemplate massive increases in the taxation of alcohol products because that would be a sure vote loser. Alcohol is a very popular substance, and commands widespread support amongst all voters. No government can be re-elected without making inroads into socio-economic groups C2, D, and E whose votes supplement the much sought-after backing of groups A, B, and C1. So even if only beer prices were raised, hitting manual non-skilled workers more than managers and white-collar staff, a government would still be wary. Ironically, a Conservative administration which can afford to alienate more potential voters in the working-classes is tied by traditional loyalty to the brewers.

The brewers of alcohol and the distillers are tremendously powerful. They contribute generously to party-political funds. More than 70 M.P.s at any one time speak up openly in Parliament for the brewing and licensed trades. In 1987, the pro-alcohol lobby did suffer when the Government refused to follow an E.E.C. directive to **reduce** excise duties to fall in line with the Common Market's levy on wines and spirits, but the lobby arose strengthened in 1989 to fight a vigorous campaign against a Monopolies' and Mergers' Commission Report that might have created far more free-houses and made alcohol sales less profitable.

This report recommended that the six big brewers should be limited to 2000 tied houses each, and that every landlord should be able to sell at least one guest beer. Lord Young, the then Trade and Industry Secretary, announced that he was minded to implement such proposals, but after a costly campaign spotlighting the much loved local, Lord Young changed his mind. He said that only half the public houses over the number 2000 per brewer would have to be released from brewery tie, and that low interest loans could still be offered to pubs to secure a tie to one brewery's products.

At such times, the observer can see one Government department holding back another. The Ministry of Health, The Ministry of Agriculture, The Home Office, The Department of Trade and Industry and The Department of Employment all have an interest in alcohol consumption, or reduced consumption, but they will never agree even among themselves.

It is estimated that ¾ of a million employees depend on alcohol sales for their living. That number, and the influential tourist market, provide more incentives for the Government to keep alcohol sales bouyant. 5% of the Gross National Product, and at least ten of the top hundred companies operating in Britain, could be dented by swingeing increases in alcohol taxation.

The Scottish distillers took the unusual step of sending the (then) Foreign Secretary, Sir Geoffrey Howe, to Japan to defend lucrative Scotch whisky sales in a developed country that was already producing home-made spirits cheaper, and packaged in its own Tartan boxes.

The biggest impediment to higher taxation of alcohol is the revenue it brings to the Exchequer. No Chancellor wants to raise excise duty to the point where declining sales might yield less duty (although more duty on some bottles sold). Already the tax on whisky is £6.75 out of a supermarket price of £9.00 per bottle. Would people start to smuggle in spirits or illegally distil their own if the price went higher? Would young people in particular change to mood-changing drugs as a cheaper alternative? Would tramps drink methylated spirits rather than the real thing? So the Government is more dependent on alcohol than the "alcoholic"!

Meanwhile, the general public remains equally unsure about **its** approach. The subject is rarely mentioned in election campaigns. It is not part of the National Curriculum. It is not even the subject of a big moral panic like the ones surrounding Hippies travelling to Stonehenge, and muggers in the underground. When alcohol is mentioned in conversation, it is nearly always with hushed tones and admiration — as an agent of peace and goodwill among men. The fact that everyday reality cries out against such a conclusion is immaterial. Alcohol, literally, gets a very good press.

Although 37% of people (according to the Transport and Road Research Laboratory) now want more police on the roads, and although an unprecedented 77% (against 32% in 1978) now want a random breathalyser, there is no groundswell of support for stricter licensing laws (backed by only half the population), or for higher taxes on alcohol (taking account of rises in the cost of living anyway, supported by only ¼ of the population).

If alcohol is complicated, so too are the young people that drink it. Chappell has commented that: "Youth is seen as both irresponsible and vulnerable, both aggressor and victim, in need of both protection and control". If the average man in the street exists, presumably he wants something doing about "lager louts", but what? Treat an exuberant boy as a criminal and you label him for life. Treat him as a waif or stray and you will soon realise that what he's just done is extremely disruptive and distressing. Treat him as an outcast and you deny the common heritage of all "lager louts": the hard-drinking, male-dominated, British public house.

So two propositions are possible: "If alcohol costs the nation one million pounds for every one-and-a-half million pounds it brings in, better leave alcohol untouched, **or** conversely: "If alcohol and the problems associated with alcohol cost the nation £2000 million each year, and solutions would have a net cost of only £1990 million each year, the Government would be £10 million in the black, and able to act."

The snag is: it takes time for some of the savings to become visible. One father might be alive at 50 rather than dead at 30. How does one register those 20 extra years of family and business life? One barmaid is redeployed as a hairdresser: is she more use doing perms than swilling glasses? One hospital bed not used for a drunken motorcyclist with severe brain damage is used instead for a pedalcyclist caught under the wheels of one of those speeding juggernauts. Where does that fit on the Health Service balance sheet? Marriages kept together because one partner curbs his drinking add up to many less houses built and many less cars on the road, but eventual savings show on too broad a spread of balance sheets, if at all.

Because savings are oblique; because marginal seats must be preserved; because most parents and politicians drink alcohol; and because public opinion is muted, there is a lack of **political will** to tackle teenage drinking, although noises will be made if young people run amok. Consumers might however have power where governments do not. Consumer antagonism toward cigarettes and smoking in public places is beginning to show. Vegetarianism is beginning to worry the National Farmers' Union. Disinvestment in South Africa is beginning to hit the big banks and certain multinationals. Alcohol is not only a very price-sensitive product; it is also **optional** because thirst can be quenched without it. Some young people may actually prefer boxes of fruit-juice and bottles of low-alcohol lager. Young women might start to shun beery and smoky and sleazy public-bars — where used glasses are often more hygienic than glasses washed in the little sink of cold suds! Holidaymakers might not re-book the type of package holiday which is a drunken orgy, nor be willing to witness such an unedifying spectacle.

Young people have power: power to get those obscene prints and calendars taken down, power to break engagements to affianced drunkards, power to ask football executives to be as sober as ordinary football followers, power to get alcohol talked about alongside Crack and Heroin, power to counteract public house racism, power to deprive peers of companionship, power to stop the party, power to write to M.P.s and ministers — power to say NO.

It was once said that reform is all right provided it does not change anything! Public attitudes toward alcohol are ripe for revision, if only to stop the anomaly that in the event of a crime, drink is counted as **mitigation**, not as aggravation. The violent lad about to beat up a ticket inspector on the late-night bus says he "will not do it again", because he "regrets what happens", when the "drink gets to my head". Now is the time for tackling drink and young drinker in tandem, each taking a measure of responsibility.

External scapegoats are tempting targets: blame publicans, or schools, or broken homes, or advertisers, or turnstile operators, or shop assistants, or the police, or probation officers, or journalists, or politicans. Each of these components of society has in turn been expected to deal with teenage drinking when it runs to excess, yet each is a distraction from the culture that embraces drink and drinker, and which makes drinkers of those same people who are expected to respond to the menace visible on all sides.

Until the **drinking culture** changes, not much else will. There is no neat answer to the phenomenon of youthful drinkers. Alcohol is there at birth, marriage, and at death, and at many critical stages in between, wherever two or three are met together in one room. If there were no motor cars, there would be no motoring problems. If there were no teenagers, there would be no teenage problems. If there were no alcoholic beverages, there would be no drinking problems.

If the said problem of teenage drinking defies solution, then it is time to turn the problem on its head and treat it as an exciting challenge, one that needs far more description as opposed to prescription, one that is worth watching and seeing in every party, on every train, at every dance, in every park, on every outing, at every race course, **in almost every home**.

Alcohol is held in the hand, the hand that labours, the hand that clears, the hand that pushes, the hand that signals, the hand of hostility, the hand of friendship. Alcohol gives the hand something to hold. Alcohol gives the voice something to say. Alcohol gives the mind something to think. Alcohol is the reason for going out, for dressing up, for meeting folk, for leaving dreariness behind. A product that is so **socially** necessary must be socially addressed, not forgotten about by that part of society that is content with moderate and restrained drinking, that part of society that is never caught out.

In more than one sense, alcohol is very romantic. It makes us view all friendships and kinship in a different light, even those friends and relatives who are total abstainers. Because alcohol is so pervasive, and youth so conspicuous, what better now than to set up a survey on the same scale as that conducted by Mass Observation half a century ago? Quiet under-cover agents, including hundreds of teenagers themselves sceptical about alcohol's properties, could sit in public houses, on park benches, in restaurants, on football terraces, at pop concerts, at conferences, and in hospital casualty departments, **documenting** afresh the process of young people mixing, and talking, and arguing, and laughing — and drinking. The public house especially is not just a meaningless hive of activity; it is a microcosm of the wider community, a place which young people enter as new-wage-earners, newlyweds, new parents, and newly valued acquaintances — a way of entering that wider community.

Put another way round, the public house confers on many young people their status and their identity. In alcohol, they find their bearings. They leave home and see home differently. They leave school and see school differently. They leave work and see work differently. They leave clubs and societies for the public house, and see those in perspective too. There is indeed room for discovering just **how** alcohol attracts young people, and how it attracts their parents who once had young drinking careers, drinking ambitions that crowded out other ambitions.

Alcohol is the most privileged Guest in the company of young people. Whereas most aspects of young people's lives invite alarm and consternation, without causing teenagers themselves much harm, here is a highly respected and influential Guest in their lives, welcomed with open arms, which **does** cause them harm! One final paradox.

Young people are already looking into alcohol and obtaining a full measure. So must we.

APPENDIX ONE

Young People Living in a Home With a Drink Problem

Fathers, mothers too, are drinking
From Intoxication's cup —
Drinking, drinking, seldom thinking
Of the curse they're storing up.

from the Temperance Melodist, 1891

No discussion of alcohol among young people would be complete without looking at extra difficulties presented by living in a home where there is problem drinking. In any school class of 30, at least three pupils will be witnessing serious drink problems in mother, father, step-mother or step-father. Another two will have an elder brother or sister with a nascent alcohol problem. An astonishing **twenty** out of the thirty will live in households where alcohol noticeably alters family interactions, and family leisure patterns.

So here are a few of the direct effects on young people of parental drinking in particular, **even where** these young people are not drinking, or where their own light drinking is restrained and appropriate to the context.

First, there is significant loss of trust in Care-takers. Those who bring children into the world, or foster or adopt or act as step-parents to other people's children, have an ultimate responsibility to provide a safe, secure and happy upbringing to those children. Children have rights up to, and beyond, the point where they can make their own decisions, buy their own clothes, and fix their own bed-times.

Equally, trust is not automatic; it has to be won and retained. All forms of child abuse, especially child sex abuse and sexual molestation, break the bond of trust between parent and child, sometimes irretrievably. Excessive alcoholic intake often has the same result.

Second, young people are often embarrassed at their parents' drinking. They dislike uncouth and uninhibited behaviour, never more than in public places where it reflects badly on themselves: out shopping, at school open-day or speech-day, at cricket matches, or on the street. Young people in any case have a heightened awareness of other people's emotions and responses. That alertness has not been deadened yet. Generally they do not find it funny when father is singing, boasting, staggering, ranting or raving outside the privacy of the home.

Third, and linked, there is the question of diminishing respect. Respect rests partly on a clear definition of family members' rôles. Mother is not supposed to be in bed at noon on Monday suffering a hangover. Father is not supposed to be slumped in an armchair, at the same time unable even to empty the bin or to turn a screwdriver. The teenager should not have to prematurely swop rôle with an intoxicated parent: bringing up younger siblings or becoming the main wage-earner.

Several children of heavily-drinking fathers may be attempting against all the odds to retain their respect for a drinking parent only to see that figure constantly criticised, belittled and ridiculed by the other parent or cohabitee. Soon the whole family slips into scapegoating the offending adult. The drinker is the cause of every family setback, the author of every dilemma. Other family members become used to the impotence and unreliability of the drinker, so that when he reforms and abandons the bottle, he does not win back any respect, nor even take up his former functions. He is more of a threat abstemious than fuddled!

Fourth, thousands of young people have to witness far more marital disharmony than would exist in the absence of problem drinking. There are endless rows and misunderstandings, arguments that become ever more fierce and acrimonious. At worst, one partner throws objects at the other partner and lands punches. Many women in particular live in constant fear of a husband's violence, violence that is more than half alcohol-related. It is estimated that marriages where one or both partners are heavy drinkers have a seven times greater chance of being dissolved. Many divorce proceedings will ostensibly be due to "behaviour", or "Two Years' Separation by Consent", but it will be alcohol that exacerbates the behaviour, alcohol that leads to the estrangement, an estrangement that also ruins many longstanding cohabitations.

Fifth, there is the issue of young people being placed more at risk by parental consumption of alcohol. The N.S.P.C.C. finds a 20% overall correlation between incidents of child abuse and heavy drinking. One-third of all abused children are found to have one or more parent or care-taker drinking to excess. Alcohol reduces parental levels of tolerance and also their normal levels of inhibition. Thus a drinking mother shakes the teenage daughter whom might otherwise have simply been told off; a drinking father knocks the head of a teenage son against the wall when his son might otherwise have been despatched to a different room. Many girls raped by their fathers or step-fathers report that this occurred (maybe 100 times) after the public house closed at night. Some reason to fear the home-coming, the silence as much as the noise.

Sixth come the money worries: the confused family finances resulting from parental drinking. Alcohol costs money — a great deal of money. The money cannot be spent twice, hence the pressure that great-grandmothers once put on employers not to pay wages in the bars of public houses; hence the agility of grand-mothers rushing down to the factory gate on a Friday night to snatch some of grand-dad's earnings before the public house opened for business.

Young people need money for food, for fashionable clothes, for furniture, outings, for school and for pocket-money. Parental drink-ing cuts off the supply of money, or more often, cuts off the regularity of its supply. The new pair of shoes for school becomes a matter of luck; pocket money drops from a pound to 20 pence one week, or there is no roast joint.

Ironically, a child can receive plentiful pocket-money from a drinking parent, **more** pocket money, more treats, and yet still be unhappy, still feel discomfort at being indulged. Instead of going without, these children see their mothers going without. Non-drinking mothers soon become shabbier, less outgoing, more fur-tive in their vain attempts to balance the books, and more inhibited at the supermarket. At first, the partners of problem drinkers treat money with greater secrecy than normal, and buy cheaper foods, flimsier clothing, and think of ways to distract creditors. Only when the gas is actually disconnected will the whole family wake up to the chilling truth. Few bars allow credit, so bar-staff get paid first of all. Larger off-licences might well allow credit-cards but one has to buy very extravagantly before a credit-card company reduces the credit-limit.

Seventh, some young people go into their shells when they witness the problem drinking of father and mother, and thus suf-fer its direst consequences. Their school-work falls off; they lack energy and initiative; their own friends desert them. They are then labelled "maladjusted" and receive the attention of remedial teachers and educational psychologists. It is estimated that the children of heavy drinkers are five times more likely to be refer-red to Child Guidance. It would be criminal if the seat of their anxieties was sought in the children's own personalities, in their genes or their acting-out behaviour, rather than in their home circumstances where those circumstances are clouded by alcohol.

Last, many children of heavy drinkers, or of light drinkers who have remarried into alcohol, find themselves condemned to future misery, to the curtailment of their own employment opportunities, or to the demise of their own marriages. Rarely is it as simple as the child imitating the drinking parent. Somehow messages are transferred drinking parent to non-drinking teenager which leads that teenager eventually to choose a heavy-drinking partner, perhaps **to reform** that partner; or else a curious inevitability pervades a drinking household, and some of the young, up to half of the young, become problem drinkers themselves.

When Anne Hills was preparing her article: *"Coping with an Alcoholic Parent",* Voluntary Action, Winter 1980), she spoke to Anthea who said:

> "My early childhood memories are of fights and arguments, tears and bitterness.... I was often sent to the local pub on a Sunday lunch-time to bring Dad home for dinner. I am the eldest of four children and had assumed the rôle of protector and second mother to my two sisters and brother. I hated going out in the evenings, fearing that my father would return home before me and beat everyone up. I had resolved never to get married and lead a life of misery like my mother."

Anthea was a member of ALATEEN, the wing of AL-ANON Family Groups that specializes in helping the teenaged children of alcoholic parents.

ALATEEN groups are spreading, and teenagers can seek help, or their non-problem drinking parents can, without the drinker himself going to Alcoholics Anonymous or to a voluntary counsellor. Another ALATEEN member, Pat, remembered this about her drunken father:

> "He took some money, and before leaving the house, gave us this warning: 'I'll be back when the money runs out, and God help you when it does.' We were all in a state of utter despair; we were really frightened. We stayed in a hostel for the night. When we got home we found the house in chaos. Dad had arrived home to find no one there, and had taken his anger out on the furniture. The mattress from Mum's bed was in the front

garden along with the Christmas tree. There was broken glass, and paper all over the floor in the living room. As Dad was now sober, his anger was gone."

Unwittingly, several children born into homes overshadowed by alcohol **excuse** their parents. They make allowances for them and filter out bad experiences, preferring to remember "the real Mum", or "my proper Daddy when he's not drinking". They idealise — until their trust is shattered beyond reassembly.

ALATEEN encourages young members to develop a range of responses to their parents' drinking. They are told to treat the drinker with compassion, but not pity — as pity is demeaning. They are to do some things for the drinking parent, or instead of him, but they cannot be expected to do **everything**, or to keep on making excuses.

Excuses reinforce a drinking habit that is already swamped with excuses: only a celebration; on this special occasion; just whilst we're on holiday; because of that big order; this one Festival each year; a hot night, to aid concentration. Children need to be wary of excuses, and of the accompanying secrecy.

Better that parental drinking is out in the open, that it is understood by friends, by visitors, by guests, and by the G.P. Some teenagers find it a help to talk with a youth-club leader or a teacher. Others depend on the confidential relationship they have already built up with dependable peers. At least a problem which has surfaced can be more readily addressed.

Also parents and step-parents need to take responsibility for their own drinking, and not locate their guilt feelings elsewhere. One boy in ALATEEN had the choice of kicking and screaming when he found Dad drunk on the settee, or simply getting on with his homework. The latter response was keeping a low profile, being aware but not panicking, **not** intervening. Another girl reported she had the choice when she found her father drunk on a hard stone floor of either dragging him somewhere comfortable like a carpeted area or a bedroom, or leaving him where he was, only with a pillow underneath his head. She chose the latter course mainly so that when the man woke up he could not escape his condition.

There are several other ways to regain control: to leave the house and go for a walk, judiciously to apply a cold sponge, to open the drawn curtains, to ask a friend to come round "collecting spare bottles for the bottle bank", to sit next to a parent in that parent's favourite local, to sing instead of shouting, to ring in rather than calling in, to hold back on the domestic chores which **help** a drunken parent, to immobilise the car, if one is over 16, to start living somewhere else. Lecturing gets nowhere, but certain actions carry their own message. It is important not to feed or to amplify the problem, but to de-escalate, and to withdraw.

Most important is that a teenager, more than her younger brothers or sisters, should take the initiative and hold a family conference, ask to be consulted, and demand free-flowing money for food and clothing. This can be vital where a teenager lives with a lone parent and that parent takes to alcohol, perhaps as consolation for the absent partner. If there is no branch of ALATEEN nearby, the SAMARITANS are very helpful as are probation officers and social workers **even where** neither agency knows the family already. As already mentioned, youth and community workers often have developed expertise in the field of addiction and can offer confidential counselling. Nobody may be able to intervene **until** the drinking parent or step-parent makes the first move, but the more people who can share a young person's anxiety the better.

Judith Seixas has written a book called: *"How to Cope with an Alcoholic Parent",* published by Canongate of Edinburgh in 1980. Any library also has books on sensible drinking, on alcohol generally, and on the subject of assertiveness. Also found on library shelves are helpful books of prayers and meditations for those teenagers who have a religious faith and who believe that dedication to another God than the god of alcohol can lend direction to life provide a pathway forward. Priests and ministers of religion usually help young people with family problems whether or not they are attenders at worship.

Finally, all young people with heavily drinking parents should resist the temptation to blame themselves for the increased alcohol intake of their Care-takers:

"If only I was kinder"
"It's my arguments and my coming in late that caused it"
"Mum took to drink because I was an unwanted pregnancy"
"Dad has been called to school so often on account of my poor performance"
"She's disappointed because I'm not good at anything"
OR
"I'm such a handful.... rather unlikeable really"

As with child abuse, the child cannot bring on her parents' drunkenness and carelessness. Each adult has the choice whether to drink, and has many opportunities not to drink, and opportunities too to cease drinking. Meanwhile young people retain the right to be young.

APPENDIX TWO

Advertising Alcohol to Young People

I decided that the best way to obtain the full measure of the assault of alcohol advertisers on young people was to **decode** the medium of that advertising, knowing that in the medium would be the message. Indeed, the medium would be **more important** than the message itself.

So what follows is not a content analysis of individual advertisements for alcohol, but an overall impression of their cumulative attractiveness to young people.

I chose the run-up to Christmas 1989 as the best time to take my fill of alcohol advertising. Christmas — for some obscure reason — is assumed by many people to be a Drinking Festival, and **an excuse** for getting drunk, and I had been tipped off beforehand that no less than 68 different alcohol advertisements had been prepared for showing this particular Christmas on television, with many more on the cinema screen and in magazines.

First, here are some conclusions on television advertising based on viewing late afternoon, early evening, mid evening, also late evening, viewing both ITV and Channel 4, then sitting down in front of ITV for a whole evening with no advertisement (for any product) missed.

1) Positioning
Contrary to my expectations, there was hardly any **bunching** of alcohol adverts. But many of them were carefully placed in programmes like **The Bill** and **After Henry** which young people are likely to watch. Sometimes the alcohol ad came immediately after an alcoholic scene in the mainstream programme, a party or a tipsy parent. Where an important programme was about to recommence after a break, the alcohol advert was the last, to bypass "zapping".

2) Links with Sport
Unquestionably, football, cricket, bowling and other sports were part of the alcohol ads. One sporting hero, Ian Botham actually presented a low-alcohol ad. More subtly, beery ads were carefully arranged round big football matches being shown live. The same brands were prominently bill-boarded round the filmed ground, in the line of the camera's eye.

3) Other Famous Personalities

Popular singers and actors took a part, most memorably: Griff Rhys-Jones. This was selling by association. Young people would see many different products presented by important people from the mainstream programmes interrupted.

4) Young People in the Background

Surprisingly, alcohol advertisers were scrupulously careful not to show many **younger**, young people actually drinking alcohol. But the settings were youthful, like a disco. Ingeniously, it was a **no alcohol** wine which could be sold by showing a group of lively teenagers sitting in a public house. Advertisers knew that viewers would have been no more surprised if the drink had been stronger.

5) Links with Romance and Sexuality

These ties were only once **explicit**. But many advertisers resorted to romance, to implicit love-making, or the promise of it, to present the drink. There were chatting-up lines (like: "Do you come here often?") some Will They-Won't They? flirtations, and some camera shots from the ankle upwards.

6) Glamour

In most alcohol ads, glamour was more in the opportunity than in the suburban settings. The exception was the occasional luxury flat, and the grand Rolls-Royce car drawing up outside the prison on the day of a friend's release.

7) Foreign Locations

These were used where a lager came from a foreign brewery or where a cocktail was especially associated with the Tropics. New York, the Canadian waste-lands, and the beaches of southern Australia were popular, even where there was "no pub for another 500 miles".

8) Stunts

Lager adverts, like car adverts, on television have become a natural breeding-ground for stunts. Many teenagers profess to watch lager adverts time and time again **just for** the stunts which include a dog falling 18 storeys out of a block of flats and landing on a bar-stool, a flying Father Christmas, and lightning striking the bar just before a man's first sip of his favourite brew. One famous sequence involves a secretary feeding a lager poster of a full pint glass into the office photocopier which then gulps all the lager before yielding a poster of the empty glass at the other end.

9) Video Techniques

People again expect alcohol adverts on TV to show the capacities of video (and computerised graphics) as an advanced art-form. Sometimes the whole ad is in black-and-white, the lines go fuzzy, and the same actor appears in different disguises on the same screen. Video has perfected the task of animation, or more accurately, anthropomorphism (endowing animals with human qualities), and lager adverts showed outstanding animation.

10) Schoolboy Humour

Unexpectedly, schoolboy humour is permitted and encouraged in order to sell alcohol (to schoolboys?). A man just back from Miami gives his mate a vice as souvenir. One man falls out of a boat into the water. Another man throws his darts at people, not the dartboard. These sequences are **meant** to be corny.

11) Sophisticated Humour

It would be wrong to assert that all lager-ad humour is immature. Alcohol sells itself, also, by matching the very best in clever humour, the sort of indirect underacted humour that characterises the best comedy programmes on British television. The stars in some alcohol adverts get themselves in impossible situations, and somehow win in the end. Memorable is the man who literally lends his shirt to a fellow-traveller whose blouse is ruined. He needs to disembark at the next railway station! Then there is the thirsty drinker who uses every device to jump a long queue only to find that the publican on that particular evening opens the far entrance first, making him last.

12) Sexism

Sexist stereotypes are alive and well in lager ads. All the youngish men crowd into the bar, not really wanting women as company except as toy onlookers admiring their achievements. The pub is portrayed as a man's haunt, and when women drink alcohol, the drink is more likely to be Babycham than Bass. A woman safety-inspector is mocked for confounding — thus reinforcing — the male expectations of that dangerous job underground. Kissograms also appear.

13) Links with Other Products

Lager sells itself **as if** it were a car, or an after-shave, Coca-Cola or a mobile telephone, so that many alcohol ads are indistinguishable from those promoting attractive high-status teenage possessions. Furthermore alcohol **incidentally** appears on all sorts of other ads: for Yellow Pages (the teenage party), mints and travel.

14) Links with the Cinema
Some film and telly ads are identical. More often, television·ads borrow immortal sequences from cinema films. This is called Veneration or Honourable Pastiche (never plagiarism!). So just before the marriage is solemnised, a former boyfriend plucks the bride from the altar. Even other **advertisements** are imitated.

15) Low Alcohol/High Alcohol
Television advertisers had, and used, greater license selling low-alcohol brews, but in fact they were promoting ALL brews.

Second, here is a summary of the alcohol contents of one colour magazine dated Sunday 10th December 1989. I chose a colour supplement from a "middle-brow" newspaper, The Sunday Express, knowing that it was read by young people, and **meant** to be read by young people — hence the quiz/cartoon feature at the end of each magazine, just for young people. To be sure I had not chosen a fluke issue, I studied the Saturday colour supplement of another newspaper that same weekend, and came up with the same proportion of alcohol advertising: one quarter of the total space given to advertising.

As on television, I looked for a **cluster** of values in the advertising, and in the editorial material linking the advertisement pages. I was not disappointed.

One single page ad for sherry had a witty caption next to a compliant dog: "His Master's Choice". There followed an (editorial) "Fizz Quiz" to win a bottle of champagne, several questions asking about alcohol. The next double page ad was (typically) for a petrol-guzzling executive car, before a Sainsbury's Supermarket double page ad recommended — among other groceries, a Tawny Port at £7.50, a Late Vintage Port at £5.75 and an Armagnac at £10. This advertisement explicitly linked both Christmas and grocery shopping with the purchase of alcohol.

There followed a two page cigarette advertisement (no equivalent on television, nevertheless appealing to young readers) and an editorial feature on Mel Smith pictured sitting next to a crate of empty bottles, having "no vision beyond the wine cellar".

The single page gin advert chose the Whitbread Round the World Yacht Race as its picture above the caption: "The world's most sought-after gin". Thus sport and brewery sponsorship of sport were tied into alcohol advertising. The next two double-page ads were for video equipment and cigarettes, again. A luxury kitchen ad took it for granted that the family needed a wine rack, and the editorial travel feature referred to presentation of a 20-page wine list in the chosen hotel.

After a wrist-watch advert, a whole (advertising) page was given to GUINNESS publishing. Very tellingly, Guinness publish books on fashion, rock, railways, sport, horses, royalty and racing-cars, as well as updating the legendary GUINNESS Book of Records. The attractiveness of this type of book to young people (who will then keep Guinness in the front of their minds) needs no elaboration.

There followed a long "Good Living" Christmas Party feature with many more pages of editorial promotion of alcohol. "We shall raise more than 18 million glasses of champagne this Christmas and drink 20 million bottles in 1990". Tips for a cocktail party... "Throw away the sherry and the cocktail shaker... Christmas calls for a bit more thought... mix whisky, and honey, white wine and lemon..." Astonishingly, the ½ page plus ½ page opposite Scotch Whisky advert below such journalism was allowed to straddle it, almost merge with it. The following adverts were for petrol and wrist watches, again.

At this point, a "Telephone Doctor" took an ad. He offered to speak on the phone about any malady from stress to lumbago, and about any sexual deviation. The one tape he could **not** offer was on problem drinking!

The one page advertisement for cell-phones (another prestige product) took a crowded teenage public house as its backdrop, and the one page ad opposite the Cartoons was for more wine glasses and decanters.

After a central heating advertisement, a whole page malt whisky ad preceded the final restaurant interview with a famous person, before the whole back page (significantly) was given to V.S.O.P. Cognac: a "Very Seasonally Opportune Present". The back cover hangs round the lounge for several days.

Thus it is that alcohol gets a "good press" even on television, or **especially** on television. There is nothing to make the alert young reader — or viewer — suspect that alcohol is not a normal everyday harmless pleasure, moreover an essential for the rich, sporty and the renowned.

APPENDIX THREE

Lager Louts?

Summary of a New Piece of Research from Aston University Applied Psychology Department, March 1989.

When the British Psychological Society held its annual conference in Bristol in September 1989, an important paper was presented by the Department of Applied Psychology at Aston University.

The full title of the research (completed as a course assignment by Andrew Griffiths, Simon Latham and Rob Hance) was: "LAGER LOUTS: A Study of Alcohol Consumption and Drink-related Violence and Antisocial Behaviour on Campus".

32 Undergraduates **previously identified as heavy social drinkers** were given an exhaustive questionnaire of 110 carefully weighted and balanced questions concerning their alcohol consumption, its effects on their behaviour and lifestyle, and their attitudes toward drink both before coming to university, and during their actual studies. Four men went on to record interviews that supplied qualitative data to supplement the quantitative.

The usefulness of this research lies in three particular factors:
1) The breadth of its interpretation of "antisocial behaviour";
2) Its willingness to compare activities and behaviour whilst sober with similar responses whilst under the influence of alcohol, or actually drunk;
3) Its relevance to the recently labelled problem of "lager louts". At first it might appear that undergraduates are intrinsically more intelligent, respectable and privileged than the majority of young men aged between 18 and 21. However, people that the police have identified as "Lager Louts" in the shires, in city centre pubs and in quiet country towns, have a surprising amount in common with undergraduates: good home backgrounds, excellent career prospects, lively conversation, independent transport, and — most essential — a considerable disposable income.

The rowdy and raucous behaviour of Aston students when sober and when drunk was more a nuisance than **criminal** — although there is always an overlap between mere stupidity and offending. Students admitted that they emptied litter bins, uprooted lamp-posts, tore down posters, carried away sign-boards and urinated down lift shafts.

These incidents happened more on university ground to university property than on private ground to private property. In any case, the intention was more to have fun than permanently to deprive individuals of their possessions. Of interest, public houses themselves are taken to be anonymous (therefore legitimate) targets.

Similarly, scuffles and insults were targeted, not random. Although to an outsider or to a bystander **all** drunken violence is dramatic and alarming, young drinkers themselves tend to attack **fellow drinkers** not strangers. Much disorder is confined to the pub itself or its environs, and does not extend to crowded market places or shops and offices. Moreover, many threats are empty and unfulfilled threats, not accompanied by excessive swearing.

The Aston researchers discovered a remarkably high correlation between the sober behaviour of students and their drunken behaviour. Alcohol added to the number and seriousness of certain incidents but did not **cause** all such incidents. Young men have a propensity for boisterous behaviour both before and after drinking bouts.

Most Aston respondents drank on 4 or 5 evenings each week, drinking five or more pints of lager during each session (but very few spirits). The **rate** of alcohol consumption was 4 to 5 units per hour. The average total weekly cost of drinking was £25. 19 out of 32 heavily drinking students said they spent "too much". 90% of respondents said they drank more at University than at home, because they had met a new peer-group and alcohol was more available.

Significantly, the Aston students who were questioned drank **for effect**, not because they had a particular liking for the drink in their hands. They preferred social drinking to lone drinking, and they drank full-strength lager so that they could become intoxicated more quickly. Drinking students befriended drinking students. They met few teetotallers; they rather looked down on abstainers; and they **underestimated** the social life that teetotallers did enjoy. To hold one's drink was taken to be a commendable virtue.

One in three respondents urinated in the street (one-fifth indoors where they shouldn't) when sober. These proportions doubled with drunkenness. One in six committed minor thefts when sober as against two-thirds when drunk. Shouting in the street was not much affected by extra drink. Everyone sang bawdy songs when drunk. Two in three still sang songs in public when sober.

The greatest difference was with vomiting. No respondent was sick in public whilst sober. 20 said they were openly sick when drunk. Only one student had sworn at a stranger when sober; twelve admitted to swearing at a stranger (and 14 to threatening a stranger) when drunk. Two had fought with someone they knew whilst sober; this number rose to eight whilst drunk.

University security guards (and the authorities) had shown themselves remarkably tolerant towards drunken students. Altercations between security officers or the police and revelling students increased in number with greater consumption of alcohol. A warning normally sufficed. Arrests were rare.

The researchers suggest that drinking students **expect** more leeway than their manual working counterparts. Indeed drinking students in the Aston sample thought they were a cut above run-of-the-mill "lager louts", although their own observed or remembered behaviours under the influence of drink were completely indistinguishable.

Overall, the sample had started consuming alcohol at a young age; they did not condemn under-age drinking; and they drank — as they misbehaved — for FUN.

Articles for Further Reference

(including pamphlets, all by publisher/publication)

ALCOHOL & ALCOHOLISM, *Alcohol and the Young* F. J. Dunne & J.A.M. Schipperheijn, Vol 24, No. 3.
ALCOHOL CONCERN, Problems with Drink, 1988
BRITISH JNL OF ADDICTION, *The Costs of Alcohol Misuse,* McDonnell P & Maynard A., No.80/1985
BRITISH MEDICAL ASSOCN., *Drinking and Alcoholism,* 1969
BRITISH MEDICAL JOURNAL, *Alcohol: A New Report but Still Going Backwards,* R. Smith, Vol 293/6553
CHESTER HOUSE, *Why Total Abstinence?* R. Bedford, 1963
COMMUNITY CARE, *Time, Social Workers, Please,* N. Murray, 15/8/85
COMMUNITY CARE, *Problem Drinking,* D. Hebblethwaite, 13/5/82
COMMUNITY CARE, *Drink and Crime,* Baldwin S, Ford I, & Heather N., 2/4/87
COMMUNITY CARE, *Not So Many Wee Drams,* Baldwin S, Ford I & Heather N., 9/4/87
FEDN. OF ALCOHOL REHABILITATION ESTABLISHMENTS, *Community Services for Alcoholics,* 1979
HEALTH & SOC. SERV. JNL, *Insidious Message in the Bottle,* Hyde A., 22/8/85
HEALTH EDUCATION COUNCIL, *That's The Limit: A Guide to Sensible Drinking, 1983 and 1989*
HEALTH EDUCATION JNL, Health Education & the Prevention of Alcohol-related Problems, Robinson &. & Baggott, R., 4/1985
HEALTH EDUCATION JNL, *The Portrayal of Alcohol on Television,* Hensen, A., 3/1986
HEALTH EDUCATION JNL, *Doctors and Alcohol Screening: The Gap Between Attitudes & Action,* Rowland N. etc, 4/1988
HEALTH SERVICE JOURNAL, *When Drink & Work Don't Mix,* 20/11/66
HOME OFFICE, *Alcoholism and Social Policy: Are we on the Right Lines?* Research Study 65
HOME OFFICE *Report of the Working Group on Young People and Alcohol, 1987*
H.M.S.O., *Drinking in England & Wales,* P. Wilson, 1980
H.M.S.O., *Drinking in England & Wales, 1987,* Goddard E. etc, 1988
INSIGHT, *Drinking: Old Problem, New Solutions,* Coyningham, G., 12/12/86

JNL OF SOCIAL POLICY, *Alcohol, Politics, and Social Policy*, Baggott R., Vol 15/4.

LISTENER, *Higher Liquor Prices would Ease the Problem*, O'Donnell, M., 4/4/85

NEW SOCIETY, *Young People & Drink*, Chapell H., 4/6/81

NEW SOCIETY, *Corby takes to Drink*, Ward A., 2/9/82

NURSING MIRROR, *How Much do you Drink?* Kennedy J. & Rogers C., 30/10/85

OPEN MIND, *A Taste for Drink*, Wheelwright E., 12/1984

SOCIAL WORK TODAY, *The Finnish Road to Temperance*, Hebblethwaite, D., 29/4/80

SOCIAL WORK TODAY, *Alcohol: The Major Public Health Issue of our Time*, Barry N., 12/1/87

SOCIAL WORK TODAY, *Alcohol Problems*, Hebblethwaite D., Herwin J., Leckie T., 26/6/79

SOCIAL WORK TODAY, *How Social Workers can help Break the Vicious Circle*, Abel P., 12/1/87

SOCIAL WORK TODAY, *The New Licence to Kill*, Fanti G., 10/8/87

TEMPERANCE GROUP OF BOTH HOUSES OF PARLIAMENT, *Alcohol and Health Education*, 1957

VOLUNTARY ACTION, *Coping with an Alcoholic Parent*, Hills A., Winter, 1980

YOUTH IN SOCIETY, *Your Good Health*, Dorn N., January 1980

YOUTH IN SOCIETY, *In Praise of Tear-aways*, Holmes, G., July, 1986

YOUTH IN SOCIETY, *Under the Influence*, Christie M. & Drye D., July 1987

Further reading lists are available from the different Temperance Societies, from various alcohol-concern pressure-groups, from local health educators, and are incorporated into Alcohol & Alcoholism, the Report of The Royal College of Psychiatrists.

Books for Further Reference

Alcohol Problems, Anderson P., Wallace P., & Jones H., Oxford, 1988

Drink, Brake, G.T., Oliphants 1974

Striking Out. How to Leave Home, Brady, C., Columbus 1984

The Victorian Underworld, Chesney K., Pelican 1972

Drinking Problems, Chick J. & Chick J., Churchill Livingstone, 1984

Folk Devils and Moral Panics, Cohen S. MacGibbon & Kee, 1972

Adolescence: A Generation Under Pressure, Conger J., Harper & Row, 1979

Schooling the Smash Street Kids, Corrigan P., Macmillan, 1979

Standing Their Round, N. Dorn, Croom Helm, 1981

Drink, Fitzgibbon, C., Granada, 1980

Same Again: A Guide to Sensible Drinking, Grant M., Penguin, 1984

Generation X, Hamblett C. & Deverson J., Tandem 1964

Alcohol Education, Howe B,. Tavistock/Routledge, 1989

Alcoholism, Kessel N. & Walton H., Pelican 1965

The Generation Gap Viewed from Both Sides, McCormack M., Constable 1985

The Pub & The People. Mass Observation, Cresset, 1986

Drinking and Problem Drinking, Plant M.A., Junction Books, 1982

Let's Drink to Your Health, Robertson I. & Heather N., British Psychological Socy., 1986

Knuckle Sandwich, Robins D. & Cohen P., Pelican 1978

Alcohol and Alcoholism, Royal College of Psychiatrists, Tavistock, 1979

Why Do People Drink Alcohol? Sanders P., Aladdin, 1988

Adolescence, Smith C.S., Longman, 1968

Responding to Drinking Problems, Spratley T. et.al., Croom Helm 1978

Preventing Alcohol Problems, Tether P. & Robinson D., Tavistock 1986

Roads to Ruin, Turner E.S., Penguin 1966

Alcohol abuse, Ward B.R., Franklin watts, 1987

FURTHER PUBLICATIONS FROM THE BOYS' AND GIRLS' WELFARE SOCIETY

GLUE SNIFFING AND SOLVENT ABUSE

by D J O'Connor

This informative and realistic book offers guidance and information in a practical style to all concerned with solvent abuse. Denis O'Conner, arguably the leading UK authority on glue sniffing and solvent abuse, established a clinic in 1978 and has treated thousands of young people since that time.

CHILD'S PLAY:
'Direct Work' with the Deprived Child

by Ken Redgrave

This illustrated, practical guide is helpful to all working with disturbed children, and describes various techniques and 'games' which act as indicators of a child's history and nuturing needs. Ken Redgrave has been working with children for over 35 years and possibly has a wider experience of child care work than most other social workers employed today.

FAMILY WORK IN RESIDENTIAL CHILD CARE:
Partnership in Practice

by John Kelsall and Billy McCullough

This book highlights an innovative and exciting approach to working with children in care, and provides agencies with practical ideas for sharing responsibility with families and developing more effective practice. John Kelsall and Billy McCullough are lecturers in Social Work with vast experience of working with families in a variety of residential settings.

TRUANCY AND SOCIAL WELFARE:
Bells Ringing in the Distance

by Godfrey Holmes

This book discusses truancy in a social work as well as educational context and gives an invaluable insight into the problems of and reasons for non-school attendance. Techniques and approaches to truancy are outlined providing the reader with increased skills, knowledge and awareness to tackle the problem effectively. Godfrey Holmes has been both a teacher and a social worker and is a regular contributor to a number of professional journals in social work and education.

CHILD SEXUAL ABUSE:

Professional and Personal Perspectives Part 1: Aspects of Investigation

by Gillian Peace and John McMaster

The problems faced daily by professional agencies who are coping with children and families involved in suspected and proven sexual abuse in this text. The opinions, attitudes and ideas of managers through to front-line practitioners will be of keen interest to all those working in the field and will further the understanding of everyone concerned with this complex and disturbing problem. Gillian Peace has researched for many years in the social and medical field and John McMaster, Chief Executive of the Boys' and Girls' Welfare Society, is author and contributor to many texts on aspects of social and educational care.

ORDER FORM

I would like to order the following texts:

No. of copies

Glue Sniffing & Solvent Abuse	£6.75	☐
Child's Play	£7.75	☐
Family Work in Residential Child Care	£7.75	☐
Truancy and Social Welfare	£7.50	☐
Child Sexual Abuse Professional and Personal Perspectives Part 1	£7.75	☐

The total cost of my order is .... and I enclose
a cheque made payable to **Boys' and Girls' Welfare Society**
for this amount.

Name ....

Address...

....

Please send your orders to Susan Lamonby, Boys' and Girls'
Welfare Society, Central Offices, Schools Hill, Cheadle,
Cheshire, SK8 1JE. Tel. (061) 428 5256.